# Living Apart Together

## A New Possibility for Loving Couples

Edited by Linda Breault and Dianne Gillespie

First Edition – November 2013

**ISBN**

978-1-4602-2377-2 (Hardcover)
978-1-4602-2378-9 (Paperback)
978-1-4602-2379-6 (eBook)

A note to readers:
The stories in this book are all true, but the names have been changed in some circumstances to protect privacy.



Produced by:

FriesenPress
Suite 300 – 852 Fort Street
Victoria, BC, Canada V8W 1H8

www.friesenpress.com

Distributed to the trade by The Ingram Book Company

# Table of Contents

# ACKNOWLEDGEMENTS

We want to offer a big thanks to the contributors in this anthology for their willingness to share very personal and intimate details and, in doing so, present a new perspective on relationships. We found it a privilege and an honour to read and re-read these stories. We also wish to thank Luanne Armstrong, writing mentor and friend, for her editorial support and faith in our project.

# INTRODUCTION

I often wonder whether men and women really suit each other. Perhaps they should live next door and just visit now and then."

Hollywood legend Katharine Hepburn's observation years ago highlighted the difficulties of her relationship with the temperamental Spencer Tracy and reflected her own belief in the need for women to maintain their autonomy. She and Spencer, as well as other artist couples like Jean Paul Sartre and Simone de Beauvoir or Diego de Rivera and Frida Kahlo, were decades ahead of their time. They were pioneers of an arrangement that has now emerged as a trend.

A few years ago, Dianne and I became colleagues and friends while living and working overseas. We met several women and some men, usually in their fifties, who had left partners at home. We were interested in how they maintained relationships with partners. We started informally asking about their living arrangements. Those people who continued intimate relationships, but had left their partners at home saw nothing unusual about their unions. They maintained close contact by text, telephone and Skype and spent their holiday times together, often visiting exotic places outside of North America.

When we returned to Canada, we continued our inquiries and, to our amazement, discovered numerous couples who were in committed relationships but not living together. Could this be a trend we had missed while out of the country? Could this be a social phenomenon that offers an alternative to the notion that two people must live in the same household to be considered a couple? What were the reasons why couples were choosing to live apart yet together? Could this be a new way for intimate unions that was not necessarily marriage or cohabitation?

As we talked with our friends, we heard from married women and men who yearned for just such a relationship. They felt bound by the ties of marriage despite loving their mates, and sharing a history and commitment. They felt they now had less in common with their spouses and, especially once the retirement years loomed, they craved the opportunity to pursue different agendas. They wanted more independence; yet they wanted to remain in relationship. Upstairs/downstairs living arrangements were not that uncommon.

Other young seniors in our group of friends who were divorced or widowed were contemplating a new long-term relationship but were also exploring a way of being together that did not include living together. They didn't want a conventional marriage or a living-together relationship.

We started to obtain data on statistics of couples living apart. We discovered that there is a name for relationships for couples who live in separate residences while maintaining committed, intimate relationships–Living Apart Together or LATs.

We found out that approximately 10% of relationships involved couples who were living in LATs. Couples occur in all age groups, although the younger ones (twenty to thirty year-olds) tend to be in a transitional phase "practising" for a more traditional married relationship that will come once the job situation settles or schooling is done. However, something else is at work with young seniors. People in this age group voluntarily choose not to live together and see it as a long-term arrangement. They also are just less interested in a conventional marriage than they used to be.

Next, we decided to find out from LAT couples why they had chosen this form of union and how it was working. We put out a call for submissions from writers' guilds and associations across Canada and the US. We talked to women and men in our own social networks, interviewed couples and individuals who preferred to talk about their relationships rather than write about them and recorded their stories. Our response to the call for submissions ranged from a married couple in their twenties to a couple in their late eighties. The majority, however, were over forty and often in a previous co-habiting relationship or marriage. They were financially independent and placed high value on having their own space. They wanted a relationship that balanced independence with togetherness.

Not all partners who considered a living-apart-together relationship remained convinced that was the right choice. One relationship ended when they could not agree; other couples found themselves involuntarily in a LAT because of health concerns.

The first goal of this book is to record the voices of those couples who are in a living-apart relationship or who have considered one. There are as many variations on the configuration as there are couples experimenting with it, but generally the pattern involves each partner maintaining a separate home to which the other is invited to stay for varying lengths of time. Often the couples travel on holiday together, share a vacation home or plan every weekend together.

The second goal is to present a new way of thinking about balancing needs for intimacy with needs for independence in an alternative arrangement. Most of the couples in this book have had the experience of living in a traditional marriage or co-habitation and have chosen to live apart. Newly met couples who are wondering what to do differently to make it work this time, or those giving their old relationship a second chance and knowing it needs something different, will find a wide variety of living arrangements.

Many social, financial and emotional factors have influenced these couples' choices. Each is a response to circumstances peculiar to the specific situation. Personal values about autonomy and family commitment have all played into how they adapt the idea to suit their needs.

Older women are better educated, more affluent and more aware of their options than any female generation before them. Many have had successful professional or semi-professional careers and have established themselves financially. In this "do it yourself" era, many divorcées and widows have discovered that they are able to manage household chores and repairs or even car maintenance without a permanent, live-in partner, especially once the children have been launched. Having been stung by expensive or nasty splits, their byword is "caution" when they consider their wish for a meaningful new relationship. They want to be in an emotional and sexually committed relationship, but still experience freedom. Many women now consider new relationships in a different light.

Couples are confronted with other considerations as well. They may have dependent children still at home who, because of friends and school connections, may not want to move from the neighbourhood, or there may be teen-aged children who will not easily accept the expectations of mom or dad's live-in partner. Even older children who have left the family home may resent someone moving in who could represent a threat to their inheritance.

The couple may be members of the "bookend generation" who share a home with an elderly parent in need of daily care. This parent may need physical and/or financial support as well as specialized equipment or living space.

Retired couples may fear boredom, decreased access to children or grandchildren, decisions around what to keep or not keep and concerns about division of property and legalities upon death or separation.

Outside the family, there are even more pressures for couples to consider. They may have built up important networks of friends or community connections over the years that they may not want to lose by moving elsewhere. One or the other partner may need either to remain in a community or travel regularly because of work, making a living-together arrangement a problem. For some traditional or religious groups, divorce or widowhood places restrictions on a woman's options for remarriage so that she may choose a liaison where she "visits" a partner on a daily or weekly basis.

The emotional benefits are compelling. Couples may see the arrangement as a way to maintain a healthier sex life. By preventing over exposure, they can avoid the fatigue factor of a predictable daily routine. If the woman is concerned that the man may become too dependent, she can avoid feeling like a nurse or housemaid by establishing a LAT relationship. Older women and men who have experienced more freedom than any other previous generation want a relationship that doesn't infringe on their financial autonomy and lifestyle. Older women of the Boomer generation, in particular, fear they may end up doing caregiving for an aging partner. Similarly, the man may escape feeling trapped or "domesticated". Often however, the popularity of a LAT can be understood in terms of the rhetorical question: How can I miss you if you don't go away?

Nevertheless, there are disadvantages to a LAT. There is the cost of maintaining two homes. There are the travel time and costs where the relationship involves distance. Family members or friends may have ongoing concerns about the stability of such a relationship and exert subtle pressure to "make it legal". The partners themselves must resolve concerns about fidelity when they spend a great deal of time apart. One of the partners may agree with the idea of a LAT and the other may have a change of mind in order to remain in the relationship. Those who opt for a LAT must feel enough commitment to each other and to their own convictions to be able to counter all these pressures.

The narratives included here are real life stories of individuals who want to share their experiences of maintaining love using a new approach to being a couple. The book is divided into four sections determined by the content of the submissions received:

The first section, the majority, is what we have classified as Voluntary LATs or "I love you, but I love my place, too". These stories describe meaningful long-term relationships.

The second section includes the difficult situations where couples have been forced into living apart. We have called these involuntary situations "I love you and I'm wretched without you in our place".

The third section comes from those who have considered a LAT, but one or both have concluded that it just isn't going to work for them.

Some responses we have found difficult to classify and have assigned them to a miscellaneous category.

For couples beginning a relationship and wondering what to do differently this time or for those who want an arrangement that provides both stability and independence, these stories offer a variety of scenarios that have worked for others. Although such couples may not have considered a LAT, they will feel more informed and perhaps empowered after reading about how others have succeeded. They may also gain insight from those who have failed and see ways to overcome the hurdles that stopped others. Those living in troubled traditional relationships may find that a LAT arrangement provides a second chance by avoiding divorce.

This way of thinking and living in relationship isn't the norm; it changes the rules and shatters conventions. It is a new model for love and independence that allows couples the freedom of being apart and the love and support of being together.

Victoria, BC, 2013

# Section One
# Voluntary LAT

*"I love you but I love my place, too"*

Couples choose LAT for a vast array of reasons.

Some come to their LAT gradually, almost surprised that the relationship has turned out this way. Cheryl and her partner Chris fell in love and wanted something "easier, more romantic, more fun. Something less...like marriage." Sixteen years later, she seems surprised by how well it has worked, and by how perfectly LAT suits their needs. They both continue to live in the city but in very different neighbourhoods. They have struck a balance that, however odd it may seem to others, works so well that they can't imagine changing it.

"I'm a hopeless romantic who doesn't believe in unconditional love. I haven't found any convincing reason why I have to live in the same house...as long as we keep dancing." In "The Daft Dance", the story of this relationship takes us through this woman's dance with her partner and how they live apart together. Nanci is a city mouse while her partner is a country mouse thirty kilometres away on the ocean. Their story is one of the several examples of mature, successful relationships found in this section.

Sometimes culture creates challenges. One couple, Jodi and Miko, met while she was traveling overseas. Miko is from Asia and has a career that he cannot profitably pursue outside his home country. Jodi lived with him and sent their two children to the local schools for several years, but then was offered a very attractive position in Canada working in a field she loves. The couple decided to move the children with Jodi to live in her hometown in Canada.

Laura describes how her love of travel and the wild country of her home state of Arizona have kept her from settling with her "Farm Boy" in Kansas. Her story shows how the LAT relationship can be flexible enough to allow couples to adapt as their perceptions change.

Other stories focus on more personal concerns. Shannon is a self-styled "Grass Widow" who enjoys her independence but still lovingly anticipates the periodic return of her partner from the oil sands of Alberta. Maisie is a spirited eighty-nine year old widow who still lives in her home of sixty-five years in rural British Columbia. She has chosen a LAT with eighty year-old Harry as a way to rediscover the joy of romance while avoiding the tedium of routine. Casandra is a nurse who considers her present LAT relationship the healthiest she has ever had.

Both Dorothy and Eileen have discovered that relationships are easier and less fraught with tension when they don't have to worry about adjusting to their partner's very different lifestyles, and Beth sensitively probes the dynamics that have forged her inter-racial relationship with a man half a continent away. Kyle and Antonio are a couple united by their poetry and the need to maintain their own spaces to pursue writing.

Others reflect the vast array of options for this lifestyle choice. Karen and Jeff maintain separate residences because they are both fiercely independent types; they connect over a shared love of Cajun culture and the outdoors. Kim and David in their separate homes are rediscovering the benefits of independence after lengthy marriages; each for a different reason needs that distance. Janette, a bi-sexual mother of young children, espouses her commitment to living in a LAT. She loves the father of her children, but, if the heterosexual relationship doesn't last, she feels likely to pursue a lesbian relationship.

The couples in these stories have found non-traditional ways to evolve new forms of long-term commitment in a LAT relationship. They range in age from "youthful elderly" in their eighties to a young couple raising children continents apart. The common theme in each of these relationships is how they have infused romance in their love for each other. All of the writers in this section about voluntary LAT relationships want an intimate relationship but need a space of their own. Like Helena Bonham Carter and Tim Burton who are challenging social norms, these writers have found a way to balance their needs for independence with their needs for intimacy. They represent a new social dynamic.

Given that two households are more expensive to maintain than one, all of the couples have found practical ways to keep within their separate budgets and also maintain dual residences. They have been able to escape the "humdrum" of daily routines of housework and yard work and avoid any conflict over toilet seats left up, dirty socks on the floor, or intimate conversations on repairing the plumbing. Instead, they write about ways in which they are able to hold on to the sizzle and to challenge the listlessness that sometimes plagues a committed relationship.

# On Living Apart

## Cheryl Cawston

When Chris and I met and fell in love, we both agreed that living separately suited us – for the time being. We had each lived with previous partners, and we each wanted a relationship less fraught with the tedious everyday conflicts that come with cohabitation: the tug-of-war balance of chores, what to eat, how to keep the house clean, how much television to watch, what time to go to bed. We wanted something easier, more romantic, and more fun. Something less like marriage.

We did not say we would never live together, only that we were happy with our lives as they were. That arrangement meant each of us doing our own thing separately through the week, and being inseparable on the weekends. Our friends and colleagues naturally expected that we would eventually move in together. While most of my peers put off marriage indefinitely, living together was *de rigueur*. When I found myself searching for a new apartment a few months into the relationship, I got questions

– "You're not moving in with Chris?" – as well as advice: "I wouldn't be picky if I were you. Just find something cheap and convenient, because you probably won't be there for long."

Sixteen years later, I am still in the place I chose. It is tiny, a garret at the top of a century-old house whose permanence reassures me. Despite decades of change, this house has lasted. Chris lives on the other side of town: a forty-minute walk away, fifteen minutes by bicycle. We have lasted, too. When he bought his current place, a loft apartment in a noisy, hip downtown neighbourhood, it was immediately apparent that it was ideal for one person, but would be a tight fit for two. Neither of us gave it a second thought. There is no question: I love my garret, my house, and my neighbourhood. My windows look out over sleepy character homes and the trees of the city park; his looks down on the bustling action of a city street. I told him, "It's perfect for you."

When people find out that we don't live together, they are almost always surprised, but not one, in all these years, has been critical. Many, especially those who have been married, listen, look thoughtful, and slowly nod their heads. Clearly, there is an appeal to the notion of such independence. For a certain kind of person, one who is comfortable with solitude and unconcerned about the expectations of others, living apart together may seem like an intriguing choice. However, when I reflect on the process that brought us here, I am not sure that it was a choice. Did we deliberately reject a conventional life out of some rebellious need to be different? Should our lives be defined by a series of negative statements, such as "not living together," "not married," "no kids"? I don't think any of these labels accurately sums us up.

That is not to say there aren't inconveniences that regularly remind us of the life we *don't* lead. I keep extra clothes, shoes and toiletries squeezed into Chris's closets and bathroom drawers, but it can be frustrating to discover I'm missing something I need. Our camper van is kept at my place (where I have free parking), resulting in a tiresome routine whenever we return from a trip and need to unload our gear at both places. My housecleaning is confined to weekdays, which means no Sunday mornings getting all that laundry out of the way to prepare for the week ahead.

There are deeper questions, too. Sometimes I look at the lives of other women my age, and I can't help but notice what they have. From my perspective, they preside over vast estates that include multiple cars, front lawns and back gardens, and garages filled with a wealth of toys and tools. Do I envy the responsibilities that come with the possessions cohabiting affords? No. Still, such things do convey a kind of status on the people who own them, a social position – wife, mother, homeowner – which I opted out of. My feelings about this status are mixed. Never, even as a child, did I clear a privileged space in my imagination for a house with a white picket fence. Suburban normalcy, I learned early, could wallpaper over any number of intimate conflicts and anguished regrets. However, the reassuring idea of it – a romance that culminates in marital bliss, thriving children, and the notion that home is where the heart is – has a tight grip on society. While I don't factor it into my own individual plans for pursuing happiness, I can't help but notice that most people do, and in their minds, my life must look as if it is missing something.

Perhaps being a woman and the daughter of a feminist has something to do with my feelings. While I never made a conscious choice to live this independently for such a long period of time, it was always clear to me that adhering to social convention could lead to a raw deal for the so-called fairer sex. While I was never discouraged from marriage and children, I certainly never felt pressured into it, and for that I am grateful. Chris, for his part, is less prone to self-consciousness about the way his life is structured. For him, it is simply a matter of doing what he wants to do, with little thought given to the expectations of others. He never views his independence as *in defiance* of anything. It simply is what it is.

While I am more likely than he is to ponder the implications of living alone, my concerns, when I have them, are fleeting. Once in a while, I wonder if I would be more disciplined if I had to be accountable to someone else. Would the clothes get folded and put away more quickly? Would those nearly empty jars of salsa stop multiplying in my fridge? Maybe. Still, Chris also hates folding laundry, and has things in the back of his fridge that would not be out of place in a museum for obsolete package designs. If we combined our lazy habits, they could become more annoying, not less. I don't mind folding Chris's clothes as a favour; in fact, it is much more satisfying than dealing with my own. Still, that might change if it felt like an obligation.

The truth is, we have struck a balance that, however odd it may seem to others, works so well for us that we can't imagine changing it. From Monday to Friday, under the sloped ceilings of my attic room, I have a private place to relax after work or school and to read, think and write (and stay up all night doing so, if I choose). On the weekends I go downtown – in summer, to relax and tend the flowers on Chris's deck; in winter to cozy up next to the wood stove, watch movies and plan dinner. He gets to work from home uninterrupted through the week until his girlfriend shows up on Friday, signalling that work is over and the weekend has begun. As a result, we are always happy to see each other, because neither of us associates the other with mundane tasks or the stress of the Monday-to-Friday grind. Over a bottle of wine on Friday, and coffee Saturday and Sunday, we talk, talk, talk – about our week, about the news of the day, and about our plans for the future. Others envy our easy camaraderie, and are often surprised to find we are well into our second decade together. We are best friends, and we rarely fight. With only two and a half days together per week, there simply isn't as much to squabble about.

People sometimes ask if we could live together if we had to. The answer is, we have: we spent three months not only living together, but doing so in the cramped quarters of our Volkswagen Westphalia, as part of a cross-country bicycle trip Chris had always dreamed of doing. While he rode, I drove ahead to the campground, where we not infrequently found ourselves cooped up inside the van to avoid mosquitos, prairie storms, or Maritime drizzle. We quickly learned to stake out our territory in this tiny space, to give each other privacy to read or cook or think, and to be quiet with one another when quiet was called for. It was nothing like living together long-term, of course, but it is the sort of challenge that can act as a litmus test for a couple's relationship. Aside from a few predictable blow-ups, we came through it still liking each other enough that we are confident we could live together successfully, if we chose.

So far, sixteen years in, we have chosen not to. So perhaps it is a choice, but not a particularly deliberate one, and certainly not a deliberate rejection of conventional values. Am I aware that being an unmarried, middle-aged woman who lives alone and childless makes me sound like a feminist warrior to some and an abject failure to others? Oh, sure. However, I could just as easily have gone the other way. While marriage has never appealed to me, I could have been talked into living with Chris. I could even have been talked into children if he'd had his heart set on it. Perhaps he could have, too. Neither of us had enough interest in those things to push for them, because we were so busy doing exactly what we wanted to do: working, pursuing hobbies, getting degrees, starting businesses, living our lives, and enjoying each other's company through it all.

Will we live together one day? Probably. I can't fathom getting old and infirm and still insisting on living life solo. As we get older, we may find we need each other's presence more, either for physical assistance or emotional comfort. Who knows? We are not closed off to the idea; if it makes sense, and it feels right, we will do it. Because my parents split when I was young, I was able to see that a woman can live alone and like it. On the other hand, Chris's parents, who recently celebrated their fiftieth wedding anniversary, have shown us that living together can result in the kind of symbiotic relationship that many couples dream about.

Occasionally, on one of our long weekend walks or bike rides through the idyllic rural communities that soften the edges of our city, Chris and I will spot the kind of home that causes many couples to pause, review their finances and ask, *what if...*? We imagine what it might be like to have a garage to store a boat in, a vegetable garden, some chickens. We can see the appeal of roses on the trellis, a cat dozing in the window, oaks trees in the back meadow, maybe a creek: a place to grow old in, together. Then we tell each other, "Maybe some day. Wouldn't it be nice?"

Not infrequently, though, one of us will share a final thought, only half-joking: "But wouldn't it be even nicer if we had two?"

# How a Grass Widow Grabs a Little Afternoon Delight

Shannon Kernaghan

---

*Grass widow* – Webster's definition: noun, a woman whose husband is temporarily away from her.

I am a grass widow. I'd never heard the term until my mother called me that after I complained about my husband's long absences. He is one of many who leave their partners to toil in the oil sands of northern Alberta.

"Don't knock it," my mother said during her last visit. We were dishing take-out Vietnamese noodles onto our plates. "You should be glad Paul's working, out of the house and giving you some peace."

"Dad always worked," I said in my now-dead father's defense.

"Sure he did, but he came home every night. He should have worked with his hands like your man. Mine had much too much leftover energy. In the dark, that is." She gave an all-knowing wink in my direction. "Where do you keep your chopsticks? I'm feeling daring tonight." My mom had five children. I assumed she meant that peace was not something her husband gave often or willingly.

By high school graduation night, I had made a decision somewhere between the lemon gin (straight out of the bottle in the girl's washroom) and the whiskey (mixed into a can of warm cola at the after party) – that there would be no dirty-footed back-talking children in my forecast.

The decision about not having offspring turned out to be a good one even though the one about that grad night's alcohol consumption was bad, really bad.

The night I met my future husband, I was quick to ask for his opinion on children, specifically on whether he wanted any. When he remarked he'd rather have a speedboat or a Labrador retriever, I pulled my chair closer to his.

I'm fine with this strange title of "Grass Widow" and have grown accustomed to a feast or famine lifestyle, where Paul can be gone for months at a stretch. There are benefits to both lifestyles.

During a famine, my sole contact is through daytime text messages and an evening phone call. It's impossible to read much into "miss u sexy" on a small display although it warms my heart to know that he thinks of me and takes the time to type when surrounded by anywhere from dozens to hundreds of tradespeople, all sharing a break or meal. One morning, I jotted down a few benefits of grass widowhood: During famines, I get plenty of my own work done. Carefree, I watch the dust collect and the bathtub ring grow. My indoor wardrobe consists of flannelette PJs in winter and silk PJs in summer. There is no lost time worrying about unwanted hair or mani-pedis.

During a feast, I experience an entirely different kind of pleasure when I have my partner to myself for days and sometimes weeks between his construction jobs. We lap up each other's attention like heavy cream and make each other feel special, all too aware that feasts, like cream, have an expiration date. While the benefits list is shorter, that list is no less significant: Sexy parties when he returns...

On his last trip home, we opened a bottle of wine, followed by another, in the den's hypnotizing afternoon sunshine. Then, we tried out the portable satellite radio I had bought him, something to keep him entertained in the great tarry north. The station played one of my favourite songs from the 90's, "You Get What You Give" by the New Radicals. It doesn't matter that I've knocked on fifty, and am as old as the Barbie Doll. I totally get this band and understand the singer's reference to "dreamer disease."

"I bought the CD and play this song when I'm alone. Sometimes I dance to it."

"So dance," he said.

I did. My feasting wardrobe consisted of a cowboy hat and boots, and a belt with a big barbed wire buckle. Everything coordinated perfectly with the colour of skin. Good thing. That's all this Barbie Doll wore.

"When I dance to this, I usually jump. Doesn't this song make you want to jump?"

"So jump," he said. When there's music and wine involved on a lazy afternoon with nowhere to go, my husband is delightfully agreeable. He is also appreciative, especially when I wear only head and footwear, and a hip-hugging leather accessory. I like this uncomplicated side of him, all eyes and smiles.

I jumped, except I hadn't factored in all the wine. After a few enthusiastic bounces I had a slight accident. Mid-jump, I felt a spreading wetness on the inside of my thigh. "Hang on, I'll be right back" and I raced from the room.

The last time I'd danced and bounced, I must have had better bladder control.

By the time I returned, another song had begun to play, one as dance worthy as the last.

"Why don't you dance on that," and he pointed to the futon behind me. I climbed up, careful to avoid squashing my cowboy hat against the ceiling.

After a few enthusiastic bumps and grinds – THWACK! Once again I stopped dancing and quickly lifted the mattress to discover what I'd broken.

"Never mind," he said, "you looked good up there."

"Really?" I grinned. Not because I'd drunk enough wine to believe him, and not because moments earlier I'd wet myself and didn't tell him. I grinned because he began to list my winning physical attributes one after another, at which point I either held out – or thrust out – that beloved body part.

He'd left off his prescription glasses. *No finer recipe for afternoon delight than a blend of liquor and myopia,* I thought, my confidence intact, at least more intact than the cheap strapping on our futon.

The best part was hearing that he still loves my body, even after several decades of togetherness. However, I am also a realist. I'm aware that when my sweetheart comes home for a few days at the end of a month, I'm a cool oasis in his desert of testosterone. After all, he spends long stretches up north with men. Moreover, the few women he works with are clad head-to-toe in hard hats, coveralls and steel-toed boots. I've met a couple of them: belching, spitting, farting, and cursing types. With either gender, my competition isn't fierce.

Today, my dance music CD's are stacked and my cowboy get-up is stored neatly on a shelf gathering dust, ready for our next afternoon of giggling debauchery. Before I waste another moment, I plan to go online and place an order. My mail handler is inquisitive, so I hope those muscle-tightening kegel balls come in brown paper wrapping.

This grass widow plans to remain one hot phoenix, ever ready to rise from the oil sands.

# Living Apart with Heart

Karen Yochim

My partner of ten years, Jeff, lives in town caretaking his mother. I stay out at my Bayou Teche farm eight miles away. He was shot six times with a rifle during a home invasion fifteen years ago, and incredibly, survived a subsequent two-week coma and four surgeries. His mother has never emotionally recovered from that terrible night, and has an aversion to leaving the house. In addition, she is approaching ninety, is frail, and has an abundance of physical problems. Cajun families are extremely family-minded. To put their mother in a nursing home is out of the question for Jeff and his sister, the siblings who shoulder the most of the caretaking responsibilities.

We live a few miles from the western levee of the great Atchafalaya Swamp in the heart of Acadiana. Jeff and I get together a few times a week, when he is free. His mother can't be left alone, so when he's not there, his sister must take over. This arrangement works for me, because I'm a writer and also read a great deal. If Jeff and I tried to live together, it would be difficult because I need quiet when I'm working on one of my Cajun murder mysteries. I also require quiet for the two or three books I typically read each week. So, as frustrating as caretaking his mother has been for him, it works out well for me.

When he's free to go out for dinner or movies or Cajun music festivals, (there are a great many festivals in Louisiana) we enjoy being together and have fun. We have a solid relationship, and an easy-going, intimate style when we're alone. We share a multitude of interests, such as Cajun history, Cajun French, car and farm antiques, wildlife, music, gardening, dogs, and Cajun food – Jeff is one of the finest Cajun cooks in our area. It feels good being close to him, and I resonate to his deep voice and heavy Louisiana accent. He's tall and rugged, reminding me of a rough-looking Daniel Craig. To give you a better picture of him, he'd have no trouble getting work as an extra in a Hollywood Western.

We're both independent types. Neither of us likes having to answer to anyone, although we speak on the phone three or four times a day, and are both there for each other whenever we're needed. Our arrangement ensures a continued successful relationship, whereas, given our personalities, living together would most likely cause unnecessary friction. Cajun men typically rule the roost, and I'm used to doing things at home my way, although I do take his direction well because he has so much common sense.

When he no longer has to be in the role of caretaker, he may live back and forth between town and the farm. Years ago, I bought a vintage 1800's cypress house with a front yard view of a thousand feet of Bayou Teche (a famous Cajun area waterway). The gumbo-colored Teche runs right through our town. I use the house as an office now, and Jeff tends his garden there. He raises beautiful vegetables, and is most definitely a country sort of person, but appreciates the conveniences of town more than I do. I can live without those conveniences with ease as I'm a throwback to the 1800's as I don't use air conditioning, and even have an outhouse, although the farmhouse does have indoor plumbing.

Most people are aware that Cajun food is a popular item on menus across the United States. However, usually the only authentic Cajun food is to be found in Acadiana. I've made the mistake of ordering 'Cajun' food out-of-state often enough to know better now. I've even made the mistake of ordering 'Cajun' food outside of Acadiana, but still in the state of Louisiana. For those unfamiliar with the area, Acadiana refers to a multitude of small French towns scattered around the Hub City of Lafayette. Jeff's family has been known for great cooking for generations. His family goes back to the early 1800's in Louisiana. Most Cajun families go back at least that far, if not all the way back to the late 1700's, the time of the notorious British eviction of Acadians from Nova Scotia.

Jeff, and a great many other Cajun cooks, start their cooking for the day at dawn…and very often the day before. He drives out to the farm with etouffees, gumbos, boulettes, or fricassees for me several times a week. He and his mother rarely like my cooking, so it's hard for me to reciprocate, even when I cook Cajun style. But trust me, I don't get touchy about it, not with all that delicious food waved under my nose! In addition to traditional Cajun favourites, squirrel in brown gravy, turtle, deer sausage, alligator and wild hog are some of the wild game dishes coming out of his kitchen or backyard grill.

On visits to the farm, we often walk the fields and woods. Jeff, a lifetime hunter and fisherman, has greatly sharpened my observation skills. He's taught me how to identify the tracks, scat and 'cuttings' of various forms of wildlife. For those who aren't familiar with the term 'cuttings,' it refers to evidence of a creature's foraging...for example, broken pecan or acorn shells that a squirrel or raccoon might leave behind.

He also occasionally sets up tin cans or paper targets so I can practice shooting in the fields with either my shotgun or twenty-two rifle. Not that I'd ever shoot a rabbit or squirrel, but I have had to protect my chickens and chicks on numerous occasions from six-foot long chicken snakes. I have also had to protect my hounds and myself from moccasin snakes while we are out on a path or along the bayou. Jeff may be a hunter, but he is extremely kind to my hound dogs and rat terriers. He always remembers to bring them treats when he drives out to the farm, and helps with their care whenever he's here. Cajuns are well known for their animal husbandry skills.

Jeff has taught me many nuggets of old-time Acadiana wisdom. For example, when you see a large flock of blackbirds, more cold weather is on the way. Or, despite false signs of spring, winter weather is not over until you see buds forming on the native pecan trees.

While taking a break from writing this, I sat outside and witnessed a grand display of just what I'd been writing about. At least two thousand blackbirds descended on the field in front of me in an undulating cloud to feast on seeds from the tall, dry, golden grasses there. Then, with a great roar of wings, loud as heavy rain on a tin roof, they flew to the surrounding trees to rest, returning again to the fields to forage, back and forth for half an hour. Sure enough, the temperature is predicted to fall into the low thirties this weekend.

Jeff and his mother have also taught me a multitude of Cajun home remedies, including herbal healing teas from a variety of wild "weeds" and other plants now growing in a special medicinal plant garden here at the farm. His mother was raised on a pontoon style cypress house in the great Atchafalaya Swamp, speaks Cajun French most of the time, and knows enough Cajun lore to fill a book.

Some people don't like living alone. Some actually fear it. I am grateful that I'm not one of those individuals, because doing so gives me the freedom to do my work in peace and at my own pace. Jeff is the same way, and this similarity is one of the many reasons our arrangement works so well for us. As he puts it, "We balance each other out. In areas where one of us doesn't know something we need to know, the other does. And we enjoy each other's company, and like to do all sorts of things together. I also like it that you don't drink. I see that causing a lot of problems for people, problems that we don't have." Although we're not formally married, Jeff has become in effect more "family" to me than even my own family who remain a thousand miles away. They are people whom I love, but rarely see.

We're both what some would probably label as 'primitives.' Our plan eventually is to retreat to a cabin deep in the woods of perhaps Southern Missouri or Arkansas in order to live a simpler, quieter lifestyle, without the encroachments of civilization. This is not a romantic fantasy, because Jeff has the knowledge and skills for us to be able to survive in such a potentially risky environment. In the event we get in each other's way in the cabin, we can always put up another one just a short distance away, but within shouting distance. I may love the wilderness, but I'm not foolhardy, and I am cautious in bear territory!

Years ago a famous Hollywood star, I wish I could recall who, was asked why her marriage had been so successful for so many years. She answered, "Two houses!"

# The Daft Dance

## Nanci Lee

In came Andrew with his knapsack and his banana. For the first several months of our relationship, every time Andrew came to my house, he came with a banana. Sometimes, all we need is a little piece of home or our own routine to feel sane. There are lots of odd things that make me feel sane too: talking in a strange voice to my cat, barrelling Punk music for mindless chores, puttering in manic piles around the house. The likelihood that my odd little behaviours will coincide with my beau's is, of course, quite low so we don't worry about matching. We just live apart.

He has a sweet little place on the ocean. It's about five hundred square feet, has a sunroom with a hammock, and manicured shrubs and flowers. His forsythia is a perfect golden orb in early summer. Nothing in his cupboards touches anything else. There are no plants and scant few dishes. Anything he doesn't use has long been pitched. There is no clutter, not even paint on the walls. The model motorcycles and clusters of shells and sea urchins are all under glass so there is no need for dusting. "Easy peasy," he likes to say. Like the evil eye glued to his backdoor, he can see where everything is.

If his house is a young medical student, mine is an old woman, bent in her ways and full of story. There are creaks and slopes in odd places. All of her cracks are collecting dust, and the place is filled with colour. Everywhere, there are tapestries and trinkets from my wanderings, books and more books like old friends, bright pink and orange for the kitchen, black painted floors in the living room, white floors and walls in my den. My home is completely impractical and just a little chaotic, like me.

Aesthetics isn't the only factor keeping us from being housemates. There is the issue of noise. When I grew up, my room faced a main street (one of the thousands of King Streets in Canada) alongside the Welland Canal. There were ships and cars, people on bikes, people yacking, and dogs. I learned to sleep with noise. In fact, I can pretty much curl up and sleep anywhere, anytime. This "skill" would later come in handy, as I would spend the better part of my adulthood on planes and overseas, living and working in loud places. I lived in Luanda, Angola for several months in forty-plus degree weather with mosquitoes buzzing around the net. Counting sheep was a joke. They had long since bolted from the shouting, the sirens, the car alarms, the honking and the howling dogs.

Andrew, in contrast, doesn't like noise. It isn't even a matter of like or dislike. He can't handle noise. His gift or his bane is that his senses are remarkably heightened, all of them. It makes him a lovely hedonist, enjoying good food, nice wine, and the smell of a fresh rain: earthly pleasures. We can spend hours in bed. However, he can also hear the traffic light sounds two blocks from my house. I'm a city mouse with a place downtown in a neighbourhood of skateboarders and musicians.

"Doesn't that noise bother you?" he puzzles.

"What noise?" I ask.

Many nights at my place, I doze in and out of conversations as we get ready to sleep. Once he's sure I've drifted off, he'll pop in his earplugs and half a sleeping pill, a full one if the city is particularly cranky. Eventually, he'll tire of it all and retreat back to being a country mouse, or I will get too wound up and edgy being out of my habitat. "It's time," one of us will say, and depart.

So, call it what you will. We like our abodes distinctly apart.

I find having abodes apart makes bodies closer. There is still compromise. It just isn't around daily domestic habits. I don't know about other people, but I've had soul-destroying conversations around kitchen dirt. Compromise is around who we are and what feeds us. Do I care that he licks his plate? Not as much as I care that he is in my corner, supports my writing, and likes to paddle. In a strange way, keeping our own sides in order helps us to be more present when we are together. I need lots of alone time and silence to write, ruminate and putter. As long as I can refill my well, I can bring more to me, and in turn, to us.

There is no question that being childless makes this kind of scenario easier. Everything is choice. Just as I can love someone without being tied to his hip, I can love the many kids in my family and keep them squarely in my life. I take them camping and rock-climbing. We have our adventures. I make them eat whole grain bread and do their share of the paddling. When they ask me where their socks are, I'm allowed to say, "Who do I look like, your mother?" When we're done and I've exhausted my limited guardian negotiation skills, I drop them at their parents' door. In a way, it's not any different than my relationship. What can I say? Everyone I love drives me a bit nuts after extended periods of time. I just render those thresholds explicit. Does that make me selfish? Quite possibly, but I don't spend a lot of energy chastising myself for what makes me tick. I just try to muddle through it.

Then there are the practical issues: two houses, two sets of payments, not to mention the ecological footprint. Yet it is, in its way, entirely practical to keep pools of money and assets distinct. There is nothing like money or a renovation to unhinge a happy couple. I can't quite afford my home on my own, so I take in short-term room and board rentals, and rent out my parking space. I get some extra cash in a transactional relationship that allows for straight negotiation on trivialities such as dishes or lights. Andrew has the freedom to pursue his own lifestyle which, again, is simpler. He's fully retired living on a limited budget, following his spending patterns to the cent. I, well, am not. We met in the late afternoon of our lives so we've both worked pretty hard at our livelihoods. Have we become rigid? Perhaps, but I prefer to say that we like our choices.

We meet in the middle… comfortably. We share values. We share interests. Most importantly, we share laughter, and a quirky way of looking at the world.

Also, absence does make the heart grow fonder, a controlled absence. This arrangement might not work if he was living in Switzerland or even Toronto, but living thirty kilometers apart is perfect. It is a short drive or bicycle ride. I get exercise seeing him. We both ride motorcycles and his windy ocean highway is a perfect transition in or out of a visit. It would be ridiculous to say that every moment is more special for the space, but there is no doubt that the experience is heightened. We need to plan to be together, and to think about when we want to be alone. Everything between us is more deliberate.

The other day we had our first knockout, drag-down fight. We had been ocean kayaking on a perfect day through a crops of islands under a flat-clouded blue sky. All was still, our paddles like hot knives in butter. Raised on the water, he's a more experienced kayaker and likes to take more risks in the surf. He also likes to stop more often, get out of the boat, and wander on an island. I'm happy to keep plugging on. So we let the other person be who are they are and do what they do. He stopped and went for a little hike. I kept paddling the bay.

Everything was fine until I paddled back to him, and saw him getting back into his boat. I assumed that he'd had enough time, and that we'd resume. He, not seeing me, paddled out, and disappeared into the crashing surf, around the island and out of my sight. I sat stewing in my long yellow kayak in the middle of the bay. I waited for quite some time for him to reappear. No Andrew.

I began to hear pulsing in my ears. Finally, I headed back furious to our entry point – the kayaking clubhouse. We were both angry about the other taking off. Who in the end was wrong? Had he not seen me because he had not taken the time to look? Had he underestimated time? Had I really waited a long time or did the adrenaline in my body make it feel longer? Was I out of line? As with most muddles, the truth was likely somewhere in the middle, somewhere between wonderfully independent and too independent.

When things were moving a bit too quickly, he assured me, "*Don't worry – we won't get married, live together or have a baby.*" Um, none of those were on the table to begin with, I offered back smiling.

I'm a hopeless romantic who doesn't believe in unconditional love. That's not the same as not believing in commitment. Those who know and love me will say that I'm loyal and dedicated to the people in my life. However, there are conditions. I expect respect. I expect something back. If someone is abusive to me, physically or emotionally, I'm afraid I'm going to pull my love and investment. If I am putting in far more than I am getting back consistently over time, why would I stay? I think we all have conditions of some sort. I believe that somehow being strict about bottom-line conditions helps me be more generous in other ways. Thus, I stay clear of contracts and promises that I may not be able to keep: no marriages, no buying a house together, no sacrifices. I am prepared to compromise, yes, but not sacrifice. Such an attitude may not sound very romantic. I just try to practice no harm and live fully being me and letting him be himself as long as we're good to one another. I've had several loving and fulfilling long term relationships. Two lasted close to a decade. I don't expect things to last forever, but if they do, well, that's even better.

When our arguments about the kayak misadventure peaked, we hung up the phone, angry and tense. I had said some things that weren't very nice. Perhaps, the distance makes it easier to be mean. I'm the one with the temper, and I wasn't looking in his eyes. So, I realized that I should take a step toward him. It was late and raining. I borrowed a friend's car and drove to his place to surprise him. He melted when he saw me knocking on his back window, hair dripping. Romance has many faces.

Living apart doesn't stop people from clashing, of course. In fact, the very nature that causes them to make that choice is likely the same trait that rears its horned head at other times. Relationships are messy and tangled and delirious. Unless we are dating ourselves (which wouldn't be much fun) we're going to bump up against someone else in all their glory and foibles. It's really how we handle these encounters that shape us as humans and lovers in the wide daft dance. I haven't found any convincing reason why I have to live in the same house, or even on the same street, for that matter, as long as we keep our corners clean. And keep dancing.

# A Lady and a Gentleman

Linda Breault

In the winter of her seventy-eighth year, Maisie dressed up in her black wool skirt and rose coloured sweater-set, her finest earrings and dancing shoes – for Maisie believes a lady always dresses *up* to go out – and off she and her girlfriend went to the first seniors' dance she had ever been to. Her best friend, Pauline, convinced her that it was time she began socializing more, now that she had been a widow for several years. Maisie balked at first, "What, dance with those old fogies?" She went anyway. It was good exercise.

The events that ensued after that seniors' dance have provided Maisie with what she calls the best of both worlds. Eleven years later, Maisie invited me to interview her and record her recollection of that evening and the years that followed.

I walk along the snow-packed path to the opened door of the wartime house in a small town in the mountains of British Columbia. As I enter, I am warmly and firmly embraced by the narrator of this story, an eighty-nine year-old woman I have come to interview about her eleven year-long living-apart-together relationship with her boyfriend, eighty year-old Harry.

Maisie is dressed for the occasion. She wears a tailored pair of slacks with a soft green sweater. Her nails are polished a soft coral to match her lipstick, just as her earrings and necklace do. Her ash blonde wig complements her glowing powdered face. She points out her diamond engagement ring, "a couple of grams".

So begins our interview over the kitchen table as Maisie tells me about how lucky she is to have found this man, a man she says is not like another man living. She calls him *boyfriend* because when she used to say "fiancé", people wanted to know when they were getting married. Maisie never has had intentions of getting married again. She just wants to have a committed romance.

Harry's picture is prominently placed on the kitchen table. He was eighty in June. "He's a young one. I got a teenager;" she says. "He has a full head of white hair and wears clothes like a king. And what a smooth dancer he is. What a beautiful man he is." Maisie loves the way he dresses and his gallant ways. She says she makes him feel important, and when he forgets something, she never tells him. In fact, if there is something she doesn't like, she just remains silent. Even though he is stubborn about some things, she is able to ignore it.

Maisie starts her story with a description of the setting where they met. The regular dance was held at the Kimberley Seniors Centre. There were so many women and not so many men according to Maisie. Harry was there. Maisie says, "Harry, being the man he is, danced with every woman there, but I noticed he danced with me twice. At the next dance Harry came over to say, "I just can't help but come over to tell you how well-dressed you are." Every week for six weeks she went to the dance, and every week she danced two dances with him. She describes how she always dressed nicely.

Maisie began to think that maybe Harry was interested in her, but she also knew he had a girlfriend. She was confused about having a man in her life, but she was also clear she didn't ever want to marry again. She had not dated anyone since her husband of fifty years had died and didn't think she wanted to. "When you are married you are pleasing two people. I have to get up and make breakfast, and I have to take time to get ready. Now I can get up when I want to and cook what I want, when I want. It's so wonderful. If I don't want to do something, I can do it tomorrow. I know this." With regular visits from her friends and occasional ones from her two sons who lived at the coast, she was happy living in the family home. On the other hand, she also loved the attention from Harry.

When Harry first asked her out, she told him, "Oh no. I had a wonderful marriage and I don't have room in my life for another man." Nevertheless, Harry persisted. Maisie decided to consult her eldest son. He told her that he thought she should go out with Harry. She felt reassured. As Maisie says, "I was walking the floor. I was shaking in my boots, but when he phoned again I decided to go."

They danced and danced and danced. They went out again and again, and after three months, they became engaged

In Maisie's words:

The reason we got engaged was we knew we wanted to be boyfriend and girlfriend. We couldn't believe we had met each other. There are so many women younger than I am, and I wanted to keep him. I am a livewire, and he likes that in me. We go out every Saturday night, and he won't let me pay for a thing. He has deep pockets and won't let me pay for a thing. There isn't another man like this living. He'd hang from a rope for me. He likes my bones. I hit the jackpot!

I am never getting married even though I am engaged. People thought that we were getting married and just hiding. He'd be happy if we lived together, but I don't want to. Living apart together is perfect. All my friends said I was going to be sorry, but I am not. Other women tell me they are jealous.

He thought we were going to get married. He loved it because I wore his ring. It was stability for him. It is a togetherness ring, which means he can't date anyone else. He wants me to move into his house, but I don't want to. I am very independent. No way. I want to be on my own. Why would you want to cook three meals a day? I have him for dinner once a week and always give him the leftovers to take

> home. He takes me out for dinner once a week, and sometimes we go to Cranbrook and stay in a fancy hotel and go out for dinner. We sleep in the same bed. We sure do, and I look forward to it.
>
> We used to see each other every night when I was younger; then, we cut it down to every other night. It was a lot of work to keep up the house and him. I always had to spruce up, and that's a lot of work. I wear an evening gown when I go out and that's work.

Harry and Maisie's relationship is changing as both of them age and their energy level changes. They aren't travelling so much anymore. They both have had hip operations, and travel is not so comfortable and not so much fun anymore. They don't intend to do any more long trips. Gone are their trips to Europe. Maisie and Harry don't like plane travel now. Harry likes to drive so that their trips are now short excursions in the area. Their usual monthly overnighters at the Prestige Inn in a nearby town are the extent of their travels now. He phones her every day at noon sharp. They talk about half an hour even about nothing. There's never a day that they don't have contact with each other.

When Maisie had her hip operation, Harry was the one who looked after her. He insisted she stay at his place and put her in his bed. He slept in a big chair in the bedroom looking over her and being attentive to anything she needed.

I asked Maisie how Harry feels about their living-apart-together relationship. She says that although Harry is quite willing to say it is okay, he still keeps on trying to have her marry him. Nevertheless, no matter what, he will always look after her and give her wonderful gifts.

Maisie's sons think the relationship is good for their mother and see no problem with their not getting married. Harry's children also support their lifestyle. Maisie thinks most of her married friends are jealous because she has the best of both worlds. Her friend Pauline knows how lucky she is.

It's time for me to go before the snow falls. Maisie hugs me and tells me how much she has enjoyed talking with me. She plies me with goodies to take home on the drive and insists I phone her when I arrive. The afternoon spent with Maisie remains one of my more delightful encounters. There's no doubt that these two octogenarians have created a committed, intimate relationship that supports their love as well as their independence. They both have the best of both worlds.

# Relating by Moments...

Beth Zwecher

In the everyday world of multiple realities, my beloved and I depend on each other for concrete tasks, projects, decision-making, problem solving, and a continuous volley of emotional solace. We consult like most couples, about meals, movies, and bodily functions. Our finances are separate with the exception of one account, to which we both have access and contribute. At times we accompany each other on errands, sit in traffic together, and watch TV until one of us begins to fall asleep. Our conversations graze across vast open plains. On any given day we may be found, crunching on current events, feasting greedily on the tender shoots of our shared passion for rowing, or sampling a selection of life annoyance factors.

I am wholly committed to loving this man because he is home to me. In a nutshell, we have each other's backs. On the surface, it all sounds pretty conventional. Yet, this current version of our evolving truth, now entering the fourth year of an intimate interracial relationship, is sustained daily by phone or email, with face-to-face visits occurring only four times per year.

Right about now you may be asking, as I myself have done a thousand times, are you sure it is worth it? The short answer, at least today, is – Hell yes! So in an effort to fathom my faith and constancy in a relationship that on some days appears limitless, and on others challenges me to my very core, perhaps it is helpful to look at some of the realities that make this relationship what it is.

I am a fifty-six year-old woman living in the Boston area, as a full time caregiver to my mother, who is a steadily declining, fiercely independent, ninety year-old, World War II veteran. My partner is a remarkable fifty-four year-old man, who has lived and worked all of his life surrounded by a large network of extended family in Detroit, Michigan. I would never choose to speak for him, and therefore offer only my version of our life together, apart.

The fact that we found each other, and continue to grow amidst these circumstances is miraculous. This is a healthy relationship, and by healthy I mean, energized and constantly evolving. At the same time, this is not a domestic lifestyle I ever imagined for myself, nor one that I will consider indefinitely.

When I was a little girl, I had many dreams, none of which included fairy tale weddings, princes or princesses. The exciting life that I envisioned was filled with archaeological exploration, writing, acting, theology, anthropology, medicine, midwifery, baking, travel, and even law. Ironically, there was an assumption that all of these adventures included the presence of a life mate (or partner-in-crime), somewhere close at hand.

I have been fortunate to experience many of those scenarios, played out across a quarter of a century spent working as a social worker. In fact, it is not a stretch to characterize the very essence of that career as an attempt to understand the abiding nature of love. While I was busy saving the world, and living out most of those childhood dreams, there has often been someone by my side. Various experiences have all added fibres to the weave: crushes, hook-ups, mistakes, murky sexual encounters, date rape. Also, there have been confusing sex with love, loving women, marriage, self-satisfaction, being the other woman, being the recipient of secret-touching, emotionally unavailable partners, misplaced trust, and learning to love myself. Many of those experiences now seem more like simple embellishments merely adding texture. Others, like stubborn skin tags, have multiplied with age, but none are the real story of how I arrived at this particular relationship with this particular man.

In 1980, a relationship that became a four-year marriage brought me back to the Canada I had romanticized as a child. The ending of that marriage, and the subsequent twenty-two year process of coming to terms with the wound I had tried to heal by entering into it, led to the heart of the matter. During that time I helped raise three incredible human beings, whom I love without hesitation. I was also fortunate to work in First Nation, rural, and urban communities. I also explored my sexual identity, and integrated a vast and subtly layered cultural perspective that led to what friends call my 'disco ball' theory of life.

In the horrible days immediately following 9/11 I reconnected with the man I had always maintained was 'the' great love of my life, and returned to the US. It turned out, the decision to move to Connecticut from

Smiths Falls, Ontario, although perhaps not made for the best reasons, saved my life. At the time, unbeknownst to me, I had a pancreatic tumour that was considered very rare. Despite some pretty nasty symptoms, (all of which I had) it escaped diagnosis, creating serious life threatening consequences. I was blessed to find a job at Bridgeport Hospital where Dr. Maria Guoth, an endocrinologist, had studied with the world-renowned expert in the treatment of insulinomas.

Dr. Guoth and picked up on my condition fairly quickly. I will spare you all the gory details about the effects of delayed diagnosis, surgery, disgusting treatments, months of complications, financial ruin, and eventual recovery. I only mention them to say that this is how my life goes. I make decisions that I know to be correct, although at the time often acting on a gut feeling rather than complete logic, and those decisions lead me somewhere I wasn't expecting and desperately needed to go.

Once I came to terms with "the" great love and realized what had never been and could never be, I experimented with Internet dating. We have all heard stories of those who have met the love of their lives on-line. Let's just say I wasn't one of them and leave it at that. In this case, a triumph of the human spirit led to the gym and hiking in nature, both of which helped in releasing sadness so that I came to a decision to continue mending my own life. Ultimately I opened up to new possibilities, and focused on creating all that I wanted. I was determined to be alone, at least until the right person walked up the driveway and knocked on my door. In a way, that is exactly what happened and when it did, I thought I was ready.

The whole process took five years. Preparations included sifting through the minutiae of every past relationship for patterns, working to change my beliefs about myself, and parking my car on one side of the driveway instead of in the middle. I cleared out half my closet, and deliberately left it empty. I even got rid of artwork that reflected a woman who lived alone, dreaming of love. In the four months prior to the appearance of my partner, I had been working with a number of affirmations for several areas of my life including one for a relationship. "I am content in a reciprocal, committed, monogamous, joyful relationship with a heart of equal or greater value." (I guess in hindsight I might have added the word, "local"!)

During one entire cycle of seasons along that multi-year odyssey, I was invited to and attended six weddings. I spent numerous hours looking at relationships that surrounded me. At some point, the realization dawned that a majority of couples claiming enduring love have, at best (perhaps in an effort to avoid being alone), a stand-in for the real thing. Over the course of that same time, I witnessed a small handful of relationships that for me, are a model of enduring patient, albeit at times difficult, love that promotes both parties as individuals, while creating a third binding entity that seems to be a cup over-flowing with the potential of goodness to improve the world.

Early in 2008, those of us campaigning before a difficult primary election in Pennsylvania got far more than we bargained for, when we spent a day going door-to-door in freezing cold, torrential rain. The raw-to-the-bone wet tee-shirt moments in the van ride back to Connecticut forced me to bond with the only other woman, ultimately leading to two of the most profound changes in my life. Alice was a rower who, after we got to know each other a bit, mentioned she had a long-time rowing friend she thought of every time we were together. She said we had a lot in common and would probably hit it off. The only problem was that he lived in Detroit. Other than a fantasy or two, I didn't give the person much thought, because I was quite happy on my own, and busy immersing myself in my new great love for the culture of rowing, and erging at the gym.

One day I received the email sent to us both, that served as our introduction. We began corresponding shortly afterwards. I am comfortable communicating in writing and liked what I read. We did seem to have a lot of common ground. I was nervous about talking with him, but immediately felt at ease when I heard his voice, a situation that is strange because I am almost always nervous around men I don't know, and especially for some reason, when I am on the phone.

The first thing I noticed was that he made me laugh in such a crazy, uncontrollable way, that I was unable to edit or modulate the sounds that my laughter created. His response was to make me laugh more. He was warm, intelligent, articulate and self-sufficient. He seemed to look at life from a variety of angles, and I felt as if he GOT me. As incredible as it seems now looking back, the feeling that I still have about his being "home" for me developed fairly quickly, even though I took a while to catch on. When we finally got around to exchanging pictures, although I felt apprehensive, I must admit he was definitely someone I could imagine kissing.

We talked for a while about how and when we should meet in person. The option of a neutral location was briefly discussed, but we both wanted to keep it real. I knew I didn't want the imprint of him all over the sacred space I had created, if it didn't work out. I wanted to read the essence of his space and he got that too. I also decided to drive, an option that I had to convince him was not a hardship, but rather a way to better understand the geography that would either separate or connect us. At the end of July, on the morning after my cottage was hit by lightening, (terrifying for real) I set off for Detroit.

Nervousness caused me to arrive a couple of hours earlier than planned. He was good-natured about the fact that he had to leave work early to come home to greet me. When I walked in the door, he kissed me. It was delicious. A simple, no-frills, full on direct and welcoming kiss, the kind you give a person you really cared about and see all the time. He showed me around, told me to make myself comfortable and went back to work.

After regaining composure, I enjoyed exploring his environment on my own, and felt very relaxed by the time he returned. It was more wonderful being with him in person than I had imagined. The first time we made love, he was looking directly into my eyes. The intensity of warm light that poured into me evaporated any lingering self-consciousness to the point that I found myself breathing into a brand new space inside my chest. We had a wonderful weekend touring Detroit and sharing physical space together. I loved that he was independent and encouraged the same spirit in me. On the ride back, I cried all the way to Cleveland, overwhelmed at the prospect of leaving behind what felt like my best friend and newfound home.

A few months later, after an equally wonderful visit at my place and many hours of phone calls, the ending of my job as director of a program in a south Bronx preventive service coincided with my realization that Mom could no longer be at home on her own. It was a low point in both my life, and our budding relationship. I knew it was much too early, but, in an ill-conceived attempt to bolt from my mom, I had asked what he thought about me moving to Detroit. He was kind, but discouraged me from doing so, a fact that I eventually came to see as an undeniable truth that allowed us to continue to take steps to grow something more meaningful. At the time, it was difficult to reframe his reaction as anything less than a rejection of me. I was worried about whether or not our relationship would survive the transition. I kept telling myself, as I still do today, "We'll either get through this or we won't," and we did.

In many surprising ways, being a caregiver for Mom has added new dimensions to both my life and our relationship, not the least of which has been helping me stay focused on what is truly important and learning to let go quickly of what is not. In addition, it has helped him become more integrated into my day-to-day life. I have loved watching as the relationship between the two of them has taken hold, grown roots, and blossomed of its own accord.

Here I remain for now, with a new perspective that allows me (most days), to completely and deeply love, accept, and forgive myself, exactly as I am. I make a conscious choice to accept and commit to this relationship on a day-to-day basis by recognizing the gifts in us both: resiliency, determination, integrity, the greater good, laughter, joy, healing, and wholeness. There is an ease born of growing separately to achieve our own unique potentials while sharing something that resonates with independence, interdependence, and stability.

Contained deep in the cycle from pre-to post-visit is profound wisdom. Finding it requires a courage that is no joke – not for the weak of heart. It is a heroine's journey to remain in the present moment of continuing to open the heart with great faith, and at the same time, determination to move towards my happy ending in whatever way it will choose to present itself. This relationship teaches me that, contrary to previous belief, I am lucky in love, and blessed by design. In concrete terms every gift comes with a liability, and every liability contains a gift.

Before any planned visit, the first step is the obligatory traversing of the logistical obstacle course. The good news is that, although each visit is slightly different, they all contain the same predictable components. Despite daily gratitude for the creative ways we remain connected, the weeks or months spanning the abyss of separation seem impossible to endure, and are occasionally accompanied by endless nights of tossing and turning. At the same time, life being what it is, one day I wake up surprised to find there are only ten more sleeps.

As the re-connection fires into a higher gear over the last four days, there is an incredible excitement that permeates every task with heightened awareness. When we first return to each other, it takes a minute or two for the physical connection to catch up to all that has transpired in the life lived together unseen. Usually by the first morning, the visit itself, regardless of venue or activity, contains for me a deep abiding sense of being home, together. Adventures with my companion, lover, and friend always culminate in deep relaxation and a sense of peace where the world finally slows to the exquisite pace of moment to moment.

Each visit ends with a sense of fullness and the feeling of the imprint of his presence just beyond my right arm. The heat recedes slowly over the next day or two, at first into the ambient temperature, and later into an alarming absence of warmth. More often than not, this realization goes hand in hand with a moment of panic when I recognize something essential is missing and I don't like it, not one bit. In that moment, I have to remind myself that if I continue to breathe, one breath, then the next, and the one after that, I will survive the sensation of tearing. As bad as it sounds writing this, I am reminded that, as I have become more certain of our investment in each other and the inevitability of the next visit, this panicky feeling has lessened in intensity by a few degrees.

In the days immediately following our joyful reunions, according to my mom, I roam aimlessly through my tasks in a typically hangdog fashion until the role of friends, Pilates, rowing, and writing resume their normal significance.

Weekdays, we are well connected, and there are so many chores day-to-day that I hardly ever feel sorry for myself. I try to complete all of my errands for Mom during the week when there are no crowds, and people are out for the most part individually or with children. The weekends are trickier; they seem so long and I miss my sweetie. Most everyone I know here, whether single or not, has family obligations. Even the dogs are busy! I can get to feeling pretty sorry for myself when I do venture out, only to be surrounded by couples and families that all look as if they are having a great time.

Meanwhile, in Detroit, my intrepid one is busy catching up on all the things that I did all week and decompressing to keep it together for the following week. The fact that he takes such good care of himself is one of the things that I admire and am inspired by everyday. He lives a fully active life that includes not only an extremely demanding job, but also his amazing daughter, parents, extended family, friends, rowing, biking, and community events. I am flattered when he goes out somewhere and comes home to call me because something made him think of me while he was doing whatever.

In my more vulnerable moments, usually when Mom is having a bad day, I am worried about the future, or when he doesn't call to share a word about his adventures, I have to look closer to avoid interpreting any benign oversight as a lack of interest, commitment, or, in my worst middle of the night terror moments, evidence of the existence of 'someone else'. I really do know we are clearly invested in promoting good in each other's lives, or as one of my sister friends reminds me during one of these reality check moments, "If he is looking for a little something on the side, there are easier ways to get it than by buying a plane ticket, and spending a day of travel to visit a woman whose elderly mother lives in the same house."

At the same time, I see little if any evidence that I am part of his life in the obvious ways that he is part of mine. I have wondered at times if he will ever feel comfortable introducing me to family, friends, and co-workers, although he shares a good deal about them all. At times, I speculate about how much of this avoidance may have to do with the fact that I am not a person of color, and about how much is a result of his long-held perception of himself as someone who has been on his own for so long that he doesn't "do" relationships He sees himself as a bridge, and as an "I", while I see myself as a "we". Either way, I don't really see him drawing me into his life there.

Because my caretaking responsibilities dictate some of our needs, he more often visits here. Friends and neighbours know about his importance to me, and some of the roles he plays in my life. Those who have been fortunate to meet or speak with him would like to know him better.

He is part of my life here and evidence of him is all around. Together, we hosted a small intimate dinner to celebrate my mom's ninetieth birthday. When he visits next, he will help me hang my flat screen television. Personal items such as toiletries in the medicine cabinet and a small cache of clothes in my closet all stand at the ready awaiting his return. His presence is noticeable in the freezer, filled with the bread he sends my mother and in the bathroom where we together installed a beautiful vanity. Even on the back porch where I erg, the equipment holds the memory of his coaching me before the Crash B's. From the boat that he gave me, which resides in the garage at one end of the house, to the framed pictures on the wall of my bedroom at the other, no room is untouched by his spirit.

While I can appreciate that we never fight about the toilet seat, wet towels, or whose turn it is to wash the dishes, some of my underlying questions are about how we would negotiate details for more than five days at a time. For example, he is habitually neat, while I am someone who temporarily abandons neatness in the face of a good adventure or creative project. At this point though, I would say, that when I accept what is, without agonizing about what may or may not be, I DO consider the following: it is a hard cold fact, that until my mom no longer requires my care, I am in no position to extend the boundaries of what is or isn't, possible.

Sometimes the only way to work my way through the darkness is by reminding myself of two things. First, he is doing the best he can, as am I, and secondly, we are not here to see through each other, but rather to see each other through. What continues to amaze me is that, regardless of the effectiveness of self-management strategies, when he does finally call, all the worry drains away. In those moments, I am often surprised to hear the sound of my own voice filled with a singular, all encompassing child-like sense of wonder and delight, as it speaks his name.

Hiking in the woods this past weekend, I found myself basking momentarily in confidently secure thoughts. If I look toward my significant other as the source of my wretchedness or delight, I am reminded that, while he contributes immeasurably to my sense of well-being and satisfaction in the world, the foundation of my happiness rests on me. Should he no longer choose to return, would I survive, and even thrive? Absolutely. Perhaps it is this very fact that allows me to keep taking steps forward with an unwavering trust in our ability to continue building ordinary magic into the moments shared between us, across time and space.

These are a few of the individual threads that weave throughout a fabric made all the more vibrant and durable because they are present. It seems to me that this is an amazing journey of learning about LOVE for the benefit of self, intimacy, communication, cultural communities, and all of life. Moreover, in some crazy ways it is also teaching me to recognize the positive resonance of the bond that we share. Every lesson has been about not giving up and learning from setbacks in order to move through and beyond. I continue to realize the hopes and dreams of opening to love. From 'us' I am learning to carry safety confidently on the inside, regardless of traveling through perilous times. For me, love creates a sanctuary, making it possible to live each day as a blessed and peaceful soul.

Like snow before footprints, the first peach of summer, or the smell of a newborn baby's head, there is something about this particular relationship that returns me to a place of purity, again and again. The question remains about whether or not this is a worthy patience. Only time will tell. I do know it is a rare thing of beauty. If it ends tomorrow or unfolds into thirty years of my heart's greatest experience of being cherished beyond measure, I hope I will always remember with gratitude the times made joyful by our moments together, and together apart.

*Author's Note: Mom passed away on July 28, 2012. As we move toward print, it is a time of renaming our relationship and healing. The saga continues.

# An International Love Story

Jodi Jeannine

I never could have known where life would take me from a small Canadian town, but I followed the path that laid itself out before me, and it has brought me to where I am today, a member of an international family, living in two different countries.

My husband and I met when I was travelling overseas for work after finishing university in Canada. I was then studying and backpacking all over Australia. I wanted to continue to travel and teach, so I set out on a new adventure, applying for an overseas job in Japan and leaving almost immediately, even though I spoke not a word of Japanese. I had been in Japan for two years, when I met my husband, a native to the country.

As time went on, we married and had two children, and continued to live and work happily in Japan. During the next fifteen years, I worked with languages: as an educator in the international school system, as a writer for a large publisher in a project collaborating with Walt Disney

Enterprises Japan, and singing in live children's shows with Tokyo Sesame Place. Then, various circumstances offered an opportunity to return to Ontario, Canada, where I am from. Due to my husband's connections and work ties in Japan, we made a quick decision to relocate the children and myself to Canada, and he would then travel back and forth so that he could continue to grow his business career as a professional 'World Champion' athlete. He had newly begun his Non-Profit Organization (NPO) company, training young athletes, giving motivational seminars and offering other programs around Japan. Also, more recently, he has been helping with relief efforts since the earthquake and Tsunami of March 2011, taking supplies, clearing debris and providing workshops for survivors in the northern most devastated regions.

Once my children and I settled back into the hometown where I had originally grown up, my husband returned to Japan to continue his work. For the time being, our plan was for him to come to Canada every month or two. We also planned to include times in Japan, perhaps on school holidays.

My children had grown up in the Japanese school system, and I had been teaching them English at home from the time when they were born, so that they were considered bi-lingual when we returned to Canada. I had acquired conversational Japanese over the years, which was a great bonus for language development, considering that I had not even thought about the difference in language when I had left Canada. However, even being a teacher, I found that it was getting more and more challenging to support my children's schoolwork in a native language different from my own. Although living in Japan had been a wonderful experience for the kids, another benefit to moving was a stronger support system in their school's native language. Also, the early elementary age is usually the best time to make a smooth transition of changing schools to accommodate a language difference.

Once we had made the decision, we knew we had to do our best to make the most of the new living arrangement and support everyone's choices in the best way possible. So, we carried on. Sometimes, my husband's visits were several months apart and other times throughout the years, we have been able to continue a nearly monthly "together" schedule.

I try to look at our situation, as being comparable to a traveling businessperson's lifestyle, which, like any routine, can have its benefits and challenges. On the up side, I find that I no longer am waiting around for my husband as I used to be. With his busy schedule and long, undetermined hours, we sometimes found it difficult just to find some quality time. As a result, I can have more of my own time and life without the distractions. Often, one waits and waits for opportunities to see each other when the possibility may or may not arise, a situation that can be exciting, but also disappointing at the same time.

Another great benefit is that I am able to stay home with my children, so I can see them off to school and welcome them home when they arrive off the bus. Granted, our current roles are also partly due to the economy and the lack of jobs in certain professional areas around here, but I am so glad that I am able to spend the time with my children. Some of the challenges include the children not having daily contact with their father, except for communication made possible by the fantastic technological advances that allow us to feel very close. E-mail and Skype enable instant communication at any time we might feel distant or lonely. It is amazing that we can live on different sides of the world and yet be in the same room at any time!

One benefit of our being so far apart is that when we do have a visit, we have several weeks of undivided, quality family time, which is never afforded in the routines of so many families who have a only short, fragmented superficial "pass me by" encounters here and there. I suspect such visits usually leave people longing for the next moment. Furthermore, again, I can really focus on my own personal projects when I am independent, and can enjoy the adventure and excitement of visits with souvenirs and cultural exchanges each and every time, all of which is also fun for the children and their friends.

Upon first coming back to Canada, there were many simple things that became somewhat of a challenge. For example, how was I to get money from one country to the other or obtain nearly obsolete cheques for schoolbook orders and even figure out how to pay bills? Since I had lived out of the country for so long, I had no ties to Canada, such as a residence, a bank account, or even a credit card. It took several tries to find ways to manage in these areas, problems that might seem very basic to people who have lived here all or most of their lives.

Intimacy also has varying levels to address. Not being close in proximity for several weeks at a time can give enormous independence and individual growth. One might think that a reunion is a gush of hormones, but it also includes the challenge of having to become reacquainted each time and getting into a rhythm, which can also have its pluses and minuses. This lifestyle with so much change also makes it very difficult to get bored with one another, which is a great long-term benefit.

However, being from two different countries, cultures and languages, we have never had a problem with newness in our relationship. When we first met, I could hardly speak a word of Japanese and he could barely speak English. Even though in the past, the Japanese tended to study English in school, often they were strong in reading and writing but were not given much of an opportunity to speak, even though spoken language is the best form of learning for conversational purposes. Also, in my husband's school days, Japanese speakers often taught English, so those classes were not always the optimal situation for learning natural speaking phrases or pronunciation.

I remember studying every day for a week before meeting for our first date so that I was mentally tired, so much so that I could hardly remember a word. Besides, everyday conversational phrases in a fluent situation are rarely language that is found in a translation book. Luckily, because we both have easy-going natures, are willing to learn and connected instantly, neither of us cared too much that we could hardly have a coherent conversation.

It all began when I met a "very handsome" boy, as I stated at the time, and before I knew it he was expressing his "dissanity" for me. After he was introduced, mention was made that he was a 'champion' for his participation in kickboxing, which my friend and I thought was a gracious term for him used by his friends. We responded proudly, that we had earned our san kyu (third level) aikido test and thought that we were quite on par. I found out soon after, that he really was the multiple Kickboxing "Champion" of Japan. Later he would become the "Champion of the World" twice over. I respectfully never compared my aikido skills again. Since his English was limited and my Japanese was far from adequate, it took me a while to figure out that he had really meant by saying he felt our meeting was "dissanity" was that our meeting was "DESTINY"!

We met with our dictionaries and continued to encourage each other as we dated, and both of us gradually became more proficient in each other's languages. We would take turns spending one week using English, then Japanese, then progressing to one month at a time and so on. Some things just come easily if they are meant to be. By my fourth year in Japan, we were married. We then went on to have two adorable little boys, named Teito and Keiden.

As parents in general, it is hard not to feel guilty at one time or another, but also parenthood makes a person question decisions, especially life changing ones. However, I believe that one should always make the best of circumstances, stand behind our choices and be as positive as one can be, to move forward toward bigger and better things in life! If we have done a good job at parenting since birth, with consistency, effort and firm but fair techniques, adding in variety for flexible adjustment, then adaptability should be a part of natural daily life.

Our children absolutely love living in Canada, just as they loved living in Japan, given that it was all they knew at the time. My children have had a great experience growing up as international citizens with parents from two different countries being merged together and learning about various cultures and languages along the way. All of this exposure is an added bonus when other cultures come up in school curriculum, because they have had first hand knowledge of the subject.

Truthfully, it has been a very smooth transition, with regard to moving countries, transitioning into a new school life and maintaining our parent-child and spousal relationships. The boys are very proud of their father and are confident and secure with their home life and the situation we are currently in. Making amazing friends has been a great satisfaction; having the space to play, and being able to invite friends over to enjoy birthday parties and sleepovers have been some major highlights. Because there are different customs in Japan where dwellings are smaller and outdoor space tends to be limited, get-togethers need to be arranged in another way. Here in Canada, it is so easy to hop in the car to go shopping or just to get around locally, especially with the children in tow. The public transportation most commonly used in Tokyo is fantastic but quite different in comparison. Still, I do miss my cool scooter that I used to drive to work daily year round!

Once in a while or as challenging situations occur, I don't think it would be out of the ordinary to wonder, "What was I thinking?" or "How did we get here?" or even basically "Why?" when our family is not living together. I sometimes ponder this decision, since an international move is not so simple to undo. Even though some external factors do not turn out as expected, greater joys are found in change, newness and opening oneself to variety and differences.

Flexibility in life is inevitable, and so the journey along the way is to be one with the waves, always moving in a forward direction, taking splashes like refreshing reminders and knowing that a major wipe-out can be overcome at any stage of life. Such an approach, I think, brings further accomplishment, deeper insight and bigger rewards in the adventures of life. Being comfortable with ourselves allows us the freedom to stretch out, expand our horizons and reach greater heights. We have our world and our lives to do with as we wish, and we have the choice about what we want it to be. To make the most of every dream and opportunity we may create instills positive values in life, demonstrates a healthy outlook, provides a wider range of possibilities and encourages individuals to pave their own way and become productive citizens of the world, living together or apart.

# Home is Where the Farm Boy Is

Laura Tejada

My soul is like my mind and my mouth: always in motion. Over the years, I have mentally and physically wandered from job to job, career to career, and state to state. I pride myself on not being tied down to one place. However, loved ones are different. I am firmly anchored to my family-of-origin, my spouse, my best friend, and my cats. I may be far in distance from these loved ones, but I am never far away in spirit. They anchor my restless soul, giving me the security that allows me to safely wander, in the same way that a watchful parent gives a child freedom to explore a new playground.

In 1997, my restless soul was surprised by a man who will not relocate from Wichita, Kansas, not now, not ever. I, on the other hand, well, I go where I will. No siree, this gal from the incredible scenery and cultural diversity of Arizona is not going to be tied down to a lame place like Kansas. I wisely married Farm Boy, who has stayed solidly in Wichita, but my restless soul carried me to many different places, until I ended up in Akron, Ohio, one thousand miles away, to study marriage and family therapy.

One of the things I have picked up in my travels is a refrigerator magnet that says, "Home is where the cat is." This is a motto of mine. On those rare occasions when I question the sanity of my nomadic life, I am greeted by my cat. Then, the phone rings, and it's my mother wanting to talk. A letter from my best friend arrives in my mailbox. Farm Boy calls every morning to check in. Home is indeed where the cat is, I tell myself. Moreover, I'm doing fine, thank you, no matter where I am, safe in the freedom that the people who love me give to my soul.

Another item I picked up in my travels is a slip of paper from a fortune cookie I once got in a Chinese restaurant in Wichita. I laughed out loud when I read it, because it said, "Stop looking over the next hill. Happiness is sitting next to you." Indeed it was, in the form of that stick-in-the-mud farm boy who is not the least bit rattled by my vagrant lifestyle. I put that slip of paper in my car, where it has stayed for fourteen years. It has followed me through four cars and four jobs, as I traveled over hill after hill. It traveled with me here to Akron.

In the high heat of August, 2007, in a wild, spur-of-the-moment road trip, I drove from Akron to Wichita in one day to attend a concert by a mariachi artist I am just crazy about. I had not been back to Wichita since December 2005. Over that time, Farm Boy has come here to Akron to visit, to fix things around my home and to make sure I am doing well. We meet for Christmas vacations in Arizona at the home of my parents. Besides, why would I want to go back to Wichita? When I finish this degree, I will have to return long enough to plan my next escape, and that will be soon enough.

Nevertheless, the joke was on me. When I drove through the plains of the Midwest, I realized I felt as comfortable there as I did when I drove home from Kansas to Arizona. My soul went on autopilot. It stopped yearning for the road. "Home," it whispered to me. "We're home."

My pride refused to listen. Home is not the rectangle in the middle of the U.S. map, a flatland full of culturally sedate people. Home is red rock canyons, high elevations covered with ponderosa pines, and places where I might go about my business for hours without seeing another white person. Home is not Kansas. I cranked the mariachi music on my car stereo louder. Kansans don't listen to mariachi music regardless of the fact that one of the biggest mariachis in the business was performing a show in Wichita! This was not about logic. This was about pride. Still, I couldn't shake the thought that maybe, just maybe, Kansas might now be home. With each mile, my sense of returning home grew.

Farm Boy called my cell phone to check in, and told me he had bought himself a ticket to the mariachi concert. We laughed at the idea of him going to a mariachi show. This guy doesn't know mariachi from a burrito. However, go to the concert he did.

One of the things I love most about mariachi and Mexican music in general is that the lyrics often center on the mixed feelings of leaving loved ones behind when going far away to work, and being at home in cultures very different while simultaneously yearning for home. <<*No soy de aqui, ni soy de alla*>>, the song says—I am from neither here nor there. This was my life exactly, but as I sat next to Farm Boy in the ugly concrete arena called the Kansas Coliseum, listening to some of the most beautiful lyrics and melodies ever paired in song, I realized I was indeed home. I watched him try to make sense of the music he was hearing, music that was as far out of his frame of reference as farming is out of mine. Farm Boy was trying to understand this experience because this experience mattered to me. It hit me that perhaps it was time for me to set my pride aside and admit that yes, I was indeed home. It was time for me to accept Kansas because Kansas matters to my husband. Home is where the Farm Boy is. Happiness was sitting next to me, where it has been for many years. I've been over enough hills to know.

After returning to Akron, I stopped by a car wash to vacuum out the crumbs of meals eaten while driving two thousand miles in three days. In my cleaning frenzy, I accidentally vacuumed up the fortune cookie slip. As soon as I realized this, I stopped and stared stupidly down the mouth of the vacuum hose. I stood there, expecting to feel sadness, loss, and emptiness at losing this icon of my nomadic ways, but I felt only a momentary twinge.

I guess I no longer need it.

# How Freedom Looks to Me

## Casandra

I am a fifty-eight year-old nurse living alone. I have no children. This was a conscious decision on my part. I love kids, but I knew I didn't want to raise them alone, and I did not trust the men I was dating to hang in there (and probably in those days wasn't trustworthy myself). I also noticed early on that there was a hell of a lot of work involved with a live-in relationship that I didn't want to do (three meals a day, laundry and so on). In my younger years, I was always conscious of being what I then defined as "free." As a result, I didn't buy a house because doing so meant committing to one place, and I didn't wear a ring. I still don't. I had to know I could be out the door at any time and be "free".

I now know one does not gain freedom without hard work, compassion and many other virtues. I am sorry I didn't establish myself better, especially in terms of financial security. Now, I have lived about fifteen years on my own, gone back to university, and spent time with my mother, among other things. Currently, I see my male friend on weekends. I chose him, picked him out in a restaurant, found out about him and pursued him. I do not use the word "boyfriend" ever. I only know that I don't like this word, and that I begin to feel entrapped the moment I use it. The reason is something similar to the reason I don't wear a ring. I have lived with women (heterosexual women), and dated single, married, and divorced men. I also have gay girlfriends and boyfriends. I've had the highs of romantic love, sexual relations with candlelight dinners, roses and even monogamy.

I lived with a man once for four years, married him and separated shortly after the wedding. Everyone always asks why: to spare readers long details, the relationship was ending even before the wedding because he had had an affair. In terms of my part in the break-up, I did notice my expectations about everything changed when I married. In some unconscious way, (I was only twenty-five at the time) I started freaking out that I didn't have a wooden knife block for my kitchen or some such unnecessary trifle. I can't explain that outburst, but I don't think I could stand myself at that time either, so I understand why he left. (I don't care if I have knife block today either!) I think perceptions and relationships are dynamic so I only have the present window in time to share what I believe now.

In my relationships, I have never undertaken many roles in terms of feeling the need to cook for a man, do his laundry...or do the various chores many women seem to describe. Still I do <u>do</u> these things. However, I do them as I would for my mother, girlfriend, sister or anyone else (and I don't do them often). On occasion, I feel like doing these things for someone because being helpful brings me pleasure. I have never really done these things for a man unless I wanted to. My current male friend never expects it; he would be as happy as I am to order food in or eat a hot dog and wouldn't expect me to do his laundry.

Both of us are experiencing the needs of aging parents, but neither of us expects the other to assist in looking after them. We help our own parents based on our own family dynamics, finances, workload and mindset. His business in this regard is his, and mine is mine. I am aware that not everyone has the financial security to make a decision in this way. However, we both help out at times, but again, we do so not because we are male and female, but in the same way I would with my girlfriend: I take an interest in her life and an aging parent is part of it. I wouldn't want some huge aspect of my girlfriend's life overlooked because that aspect is part of what I see when I "see her". Thus, I don't see these issues as "over there somewhere – to be taken care of" as much as I see them as part of the whole person.

This relationship is the healthiest I have ever had. We seldom argue whereas my past relationships were chaotic, argumentative and filled with insecurity. Perhaps we are so laid back because of my generation, stage in life, or past experiences. However, I would not give up what I have now for that "passionate, sexually heightened buzz" which I used to seek and feel when I was dating in Vancouver. Would it all change if we lived seven days a week together? I somehow think not, but of course, I could be wrong. He finds it actually embarrassing the odd time I've done his laundry or some other domestic chore. I think his reaction may be what it is because he has, for the most part, lived alone.

For me, "exciting passionate sexual affairs" exist along with loneliness, insecurity, sadness, depression and yes, some feelings of being alive. Sometimes, I think the cause is nothing but being a horny rabbit. This kind of stimulation has its place because one feels beautiful (even if one is hearing false flattery), and as a result, alive and charged up. Still, there are other things I also want in relationships. I don't think this kind of excitement is enough for me. Relationships end, and they end quickly, if one wants a steady diet of such superficial thrills. My belief is that dating is based on projection. One projects onto the other person the fantasy one is dreaming of and vice versa. Ultimately, I think people are dating themselves. Only later do truths reveal themselves when perceptions about the individual's true character become apparent. Then, it's either worth "hanging in there" and really knowing what the other person thinks and feels, or it's not. Each must make the choice.

It also takes major energy to dress up for a first date, or a second for that matter. I like having long periods of not having to. I am most comfortable in jeans and a t-shirt. I kind of think one must at least wear lipstick for a hot date in Vancouver.

Perhaps it is because I had "only these relationships" for many years that I can enjoy what I have now, and I say "now," as today I know every relationship can change. I have passionate moments with my current friend but they are intertwined with compassion, affection, and reliability. Our relationship is so much more than "meeting dazzling eyes over dinner". When I had dazzling eyes and sexually heightened experiences, that's *all* I had, and often I didn't even know where the man lived, or if I would see him again. Now that I'm older, I don't have the energy for wondering where a man is anymore. I would more likely wonder if my geraniums would grow this summer. I don't think these issues end up being male/female nor black/white. I think people's life experiences are always changing. I think "doing good for others has its own rewards" as Buddhists suggest, and perhaps that "overdoing good for someone" is merely self-serving.

My hunch is that my sister's generation, who are a wee bit older than I am, got stuck in these roles more than mine did. There's no wonder they want to escape them now or work to distance themselves from these expectations. I also work erratic hours and always have, so perhaps I have never lived the "nine-to-five-dinner-on-the-table life", a reality which sounds actually horrible. However, I don't think relationships have to be set up this way.

Nevertheless, I still have unsettling thoughts. On occasion, though seldom, I will get lonely in the evening. I then wonder, "Should I be living with my friend?". On another occasion I might worry about my future stability or financial security, because, unlike some other women, I did not focus on buying a house or putting money in a pot together with some man. There are certainly disadvantages to this lifestyle, but I do notice that even rich people still worry about these things.

I also notice in my older years that, when my friend turns on the television or goes on the computer or does something that would not be my choice of the moment, he feels fine if I just check out to my garden, meet a friend or do whatever I feel like doing. He isn't threatened by my independence. He isn't a needy man, currently anyway. To me, he is so intellectually fascinating that I feel lucky. My hunch is that he also enjoys time away from me on some afternoons. That is just human nature, I think. However, I can identify with the anxiety that some women feel living with men. Even my childless friends, who remained single a long time, and who never married but are now living with men, experience some of this tension. Even with this wonderful man in my life, I can experience a "drowning of who I am" if we are together every moment of the weekend or on a trip. However, I do believe this "loss of self" would occur with a female house partner too.

Yet, I can catch myself now. If I find I am not taking initiative in terms of choices or activities, I say so, offer another suggestion or just, quite frankly, "take off somewhere". He doesn't seem to hold this behaviour against me, and perhaps I am secure enough not to care too much about what he thinks. In my younger years, this attitude would have posed a problem. I would have had an angry, childish, selfish moment or fit resulting from boredom, but years on my own and the cold steel, raw memory of years of loneliness have taught me that this problem is for me, and no one else, to resolve. After all, boredom can occur when one is alone or with someone else.

Now I remedy a feeling of boredom quickly by taking initiative to enjoy some wonderful moment life can offer. After all, there is always another friend to make, or a flower to grow, beautiful music to hear, or a letter to be written. I occasionally fail to remember this truth, but I have come to believe that boredom is within the person feeling it. No one else is causing whatever it is that's missing. I also believe one has to "bring to the relationship something other than the relationship" from one's own experiences in the world and that loneliness, depression, joy, and security are all part of human experience. We can't be free of it all, or we'd never know the contrary feeling.

Am I happier now than in my youth? I can't say "yes" immediately as too many sorrows unrelated to partnership come with aging. We lose loved ones and have health concerns. Perhaps some dreams aren't fulfilled in quite as big a way as we had hoped, or at least these dreams have had to be modified. Nursing reminds me everyday of how life can turn on a moment.

Would I live with someone? Yes, I would, but I would leave if the relationship changed (and it could), and I would never cook dinner, do laundry or shop unless I wanted to (or had to) in terms of that other person, whether male or female. Having been dumped on occasion, I have come to a viscerally wrenching realization that a relationship can end at anytime due to health reasons (nursing has helped here) conflict, or lack of interest. As a consequence, I am more appreciative of whomever I'm around. I am definitely more compassionate and less ego-centered than I was when I was younger.

I believe we are like a puzzle: all these parts to us – aging parents, different men, women, children and experiences in our lives – are put in a context. However, at anytime, a piece may fall out and we must acquire another puzzle or change another piece or two. It's just life, I think. We adapt; we must.

# Intimate Distance

Dorothy Purge

It was dark soon after the passengers had cleared immigration and we had collected our luggage.

*"I've got my suitcase, that's one; my camera bag, that's two; and my handbag, that's three. Great! I have got everything. And now, I have arrived in this big city.*

*But wait a minute; jet lag has got the better of me. I can't believe that I am hauling my suitcase and struggling with my hand luggage and handbag at the same time that I am pushing an empty trolley!*

*Oh me, oh my! No wonder a few passengers have given me 'raised eye-brows!"*

*"I must have seemed like the farmer who was carrying his donkey!"*

I was walking to the airport's pick-up area when suddenly I remembered haunting stories about big cities.

*"Got to be careful."* I warned myself.

Quickly, I returned inside the building and waited for my husband behind the glass doors. I huddled between my pieces of luggage and firmly clutched my handbag.

"Linda! Is that you Linda?" Paul was bursting with laughter – just the kind I wanted to feel after not seeing my husband for four years. I tightened in the warmth of his huge embrace. We were together again.

"You look so good, girl!"

We kissed on the cheeks – just like a brother and sister would have done.

I returned the compliment. "You look great yourself."

"I am glad that you have dressed warm for the weather."

"Oh yes, I checked the Internet to know what the weather was like here. Have you forgotten that I get cold quite easily?"

"I have forgotten nothing about you sweetie, nothing at all."

We were on our way to Paul's house. His hand gently touched my shoulder as I sat quite dignified. I felt his gaze every so often. I was thankful that most of my time on the aircraft had been spent reflecting on the sixteen years that Paul and I had spent together, and more so on thoughts about our lovely children, three sons and a daughter. Still, at this point I was confronted with mixed expectations about my visit.

While growing up in our marriage we had fun, lots of it. Paul had worked as a top merchandise salesman at a prestigious car company and though I was not a job-hopper, I had switched vocations on a few occasions to satisfy the needs of my husband and children. Before we were married I knew what position I would take in Paul's life – second place. Sports, cricket in particular, was his first love, and horseracing was in third place.

Paul's weekends were taken up with his sports activities. Although he disagreed, I had always felt that he should have spent more time with the children. I remembered when our youngest son Aron was a toddler. Paul typically disappeared on weekends to play cricket. One day Aron glimpsed his dad leaving the house and asked, "Mom, who is that man?"

On his horse racing days, as Paul was leaving home I would say to him, "Be careful how you bet on the horses. You could lose your shirt".

After sixteen years in his job, Paul was made redundant. There was nothing that I could have done to make him seek another job. He felt that he had reached the end of a road. This event commenced the deterioration of our marriage. I was working so hard that at one point I had two full-time jobs. The relationship got progressively worse. We spoke to each other only when it was extremely necessary. We started playing a game: Apart-Together, Together-Apart on and on, trapping ourselves more and more.

Frankly, I assumed Paul was too proud to 'put his hands' to anything from which he could continue to earn an honest living. Even though we lived in a family house where we had neither rent nor a mortgage to pay, the bills were pretty tough and in a short time, Paul's redundancy funds had evaporated.

Time crawled. At nights I prayed that daylight would come quickly so that I could see the problems more clearly, and when it was daylight, I prayed that night would come quickly so that I could get away from the problems.

Like magic, Paul landed overseas in North America, and around the same time, I moved as well.

Grief! I was certain that our game had ended bitterly: "Apart."

Paul telephoned the children every day and he faithfully sent money home for them so that they could complete their education. He also stayed in contact with me though I did not entertain many of his conversations.

And so after four years, at his invitation I was visiting Paul. "I love your home," I said. "Everything here is clean and in the right place." However, during the tour of his house, I felt paralyzed when I noticed that there was only one bedroom.

When I went to the bathroom, not only did I shut the door, but also I locked it. I was confronting my deepest fear: being locked in a bathroom and for some reason being unable to get the door opened. For that reason, our family had never locked bathroom doors in our house, but now I had to break the rule. I was figuring Paul would enter and get really intimate with me! My thoughts became panicky and confused.

*"Where was I going to sleep? No. Where was Paul going to sleep? On the sofa, of course!"*

"I see that you have carried only one suitcase dear," Paul interrupted.

"Yep! I am travelling light these days and why would I need more than one anyway? Anyway, remember that I have my carry-on bag."

"Whew!" I gasped as Paul opened the closet doors. "Paul Finnigan! Are you mad? What the heck is all this?"

"Well Linda, I have my money and I will buy my children and my dear wife whatever they want and whatever they do not want. No one can prevent me from doing that. Furthermore you always told me that when I bet on horses 'I could lose my shirt.' Now Linda, look around in this other closet. It is not possible for you to count all my shirts!"

"Ahem." I shook my head from side to side as I looked at what appeared to be "Paul's Garment Factory" and I thought:

*"There he goes! Those who money and vanity have joined together let no man put asunder."*

My outbursts and Paul's responses quickly reminded me that from the time our 'Together-Apart' game had begun; the maximum time that we could spend together successfully was three hours. Still, I did not want to spoil the trip. After all, I had appreciated his invitation and was happy to see him.

"Let's eat sweetheart. I prepared fish. I know that's your favourite. Isn't it?"

"Thank you," I said, respectfully, "but you sit and please let me serve."

"No, I will serve," said Paul. "You sit. You still enjoy being on your feet, eh?"

"I can see that you have learnt to be on your feet too, other than with a cricket bat."

"Well, yes. I manage, you know. But I wonder why we both want to be on our feet and neither of us wants to be served?"

"That's because we both live alone, Paul." No sooner had I said those words than a trickle of guilt ran through my body though I could not explain why. I delved into the escovitched fish, and we prattled on about delightful memories, mostly about our friends with whom we had grown up when our children were in primary schools. We laughed a lot but I could not avoid thinking of what was going to happen after dinner that night.

*"How could I sleep with Paul tonight? It's like our first date. Absence makes hearts wander!"*

Indeed it was like our first date. I got the bedroom with the huge king-size bed while Paul snored on the sofa. Moreover, I locked the bedroom door!

Since that trip to North America, Paul and I have grown closer. I have made subsequent visits and he has been home too. It's more fun when he visits me. We race to the shower, and I enjoy peeping at him while he bathes alone. I have become more relaxed and loving though his love is possessive, even overwhelming.

His 'chuuupps' come by telephone at least once per day, but he wakes me up too early or calls me when he has reached home from work, and I am still on my job. He knows I hate those things but he refuses to change his selfishness. We continue to play the game 'Apart-Together.' We have opted to grow and that is why we live apart so that we can be together, but at an intimate distance.

Paul is always talking loudly and at top speed about his favourite sports. He always finds something to hammer or to use as a tool. I continue to brainstorm about new writing projects, experiment in cooking new dishes and keep reassuring myself that 'Tomorrow I will get organized'.

Paul remains like a riot and I remain in quiet chaos. I do not entertain negative criticisms from the children about their dad. All grown-up now, they always give the impression that all is well with Mom and Dad.

# Together but Separate

Eileen Ladin-Panzer

It was 1977, and for me, the dawn of a new day. The world was beyond the Age of Aquarius, and it was the heyday of the disco scene. I was newly divorced, and all manner of exciting experiences awaited me. At least, that is what I thought before I began the grueling, discomfiting world of the newly single. How to begin? How would I meet eligible men?

Well, it was pretty difficult, considering that the circles in which I traveled were conservative and very married. I had not known a single man in the nineteen years I had been married, nor did any of my friends know eligible bachelors. So, I began to attend singles dances, usually with a friend, but sometimes alone. Mostly, these were depressing affairs, with women outnumbering men by a large margin. Most of the women seemed overweight and desperate, and most of the men seemed downtrodden and cavalier.

After a while, I noticed something else. Most of the people, especially the men, seemed to be at every dance, spouting their tired pickup lines at whoever would listen. After a few listless dates, and a few encounters with men of the wrong kind, I was pretty sure that this avenue would not work.

Next, I tried the bars. That was even worse. The women seemed the same, albeit a little boozier, and the pickup lines of the men seemed even worse. I was pretty tired of reciting name, rank and serial number and my birth sign. What ended my career in the bars was the night that I went out alone, slipped onto a bar stool and ordered my drink. Seated next to me was a man of about forty with a slight accent. He was average in looks and body build, but was unappealing because of the neediness I sensed in him. I tried to move away by walking around the bar and taking a seat next to a woman with whom I struck up a conversation. No vacant seat was available, so he stood behind my stool and breathed in my ear.

Deciding that this evening was going to be another in a long line of duds, I left and went to my car. I noticed him behind me and with a sense of unease, started my car and speedily drove out of the lot. Looking into my rearview mirror, I saw that he was behind me! Fighting a sense of panic, I drove home, seeing his headlights in my rearview mirror the entire way. Once home, I bolted from the car and locked myself into the house. Since I live in a cul-de-sac, he did not come onto my driveway but remained parked in its circle for some time, as I periodically peeked out the window and wondered whether to call the police. Eventually, the car left, and I breathed a long sigh of relief. So much for the bar scene!

Disgusted with the entire, single, disco world, I retreated into home and myself. No longer did I have to hear the comments from my teen-age daughter that I was competing with her and her friends. Breathing a sigh of relief, I took some time off to see old friends, go to movies, and forget the fact that I was now a single woman.

After about six months, I began to get restless and decided that I would go to one more singles dance before I gave the whole thing up forever. What could it hurt? On a hot, early September night in 1979, I went downtown to the Gold Coast neighborhood of Chicago, a truly "happening" place where people seemed always to be in a party mood.

Standing around watching a now familiar scene at the dance, I heard a voice next to me ask, "Want to dance?" I followed him onto the floor, where we did some fairly energetic gyrations that passed for a dance. At the end of a couple of those numbers, sweating slightly, we stopped and began a conversation. The young man was of medium height, with brown hair, blue eyes, and glasses – pleasant enough looking. He seemed very intense and spoke about automobiles and all his problems fixing them. No, he was not a mechanic but merely someone who enjoyed tinkering with cars. I listened and smiled politely, even though I did not have the slightest idea of what he was talking about. When he asked for my telephone number, I gave it to him, not knowing whether I would in fact ever hear from him. If not, it would be just another wasted evening, but I vowed, it would be the last one I would spend this way.

About a week later, he called. We went to dinner, and this time, he talked about himself and about relationships and their difficulties. I learned that he was divorced after a six-year marriage and had no children. He also talked about a failed, intense romance, which he had taken more seriously than his girlfriend. A complicating factor had been that both had been married to other people at the time. Although this relationship had failed, it also signaled the end of his marriage. I noticed sincerity and something else that struck a chord: a willingness to pursue the meanings of relationships.

We went out again several times. Although he was unfailingly kind, he was extremely particular in ways that seemed odd to me. When I stepped into his car, he was quick to point out that I must put my feet on the mat and not touch the carpet. He wiped the seats before being seated in a restaurant and made a habit of wiping off my kitchen chair before sitting on it. When I knew him a bit better, he informed me that my kitchen was greasy and pointed out all the ways he found it to be so. My housekeeping, he said, was not up to his standards.

His house was not up to my standards either because it looked as though its occupants were either moving in or moving out. Some years before, he had begun to strip the kitchen for painting, and that is the way I found it. The light switch did not work unless it was touched "just so." The dining room was used as a storeroom for automobile parts, and the kitchen table was storage space for bills and important papers. This was fine, he said, because everything was stacked square and parallel.

The house was a nineteen sixties bi-level and still had its original linoleum, now faded and cracked. There was plenty of dust around, and I was told this was fine as long as nobody streaked it. When one cleaned, it was important to clean everything; there was no middle ground. Either the job was done properly, or not at all.

I sensed discrepancies in his reasoning. One could never sit on an upholstered chair or couch without a covering because there were always smells from the body or hair. He elected to do virtually no house cleaning at all because, he explained, life had taken from him the desire to live the way he knew he should. I knew that he was telling the truth about his standards because in his basement I saw that, when detailing an automobile, he had taken out every last part of the inside, including the screws, and laid all of it neatly on the basement floor.

I am not the sort of housekeeper that he envisioned the woman in his life to be. It is important to me that my home be clean and not shabby. Although not overly materialistic, I like my surroundings to be pleasant. He simply did not care, at least about appearances. Because he still had a dial phone in his kitchen and never bothered to plug in the telephone answering machine he had bought, I joked that if the consumer economy had to depend on him, we would still be using Baby Brownie cameras. Obviously, we were not candidates for living together, but somehow we stayed together – separate but together.

There were other differences. He is much more frugal than I am. Actually, frugality is just part of who he is. It is not something that he studies or works at, nor does he ever feel deprived while being extremely careful about expenditures. When I was first divorced, my finances were in a shambles, and he paid for any trips we took. Because he is admittedly more knowledgeable about finance than I am, whatever he deems fair about money I must accept.

Not surprisingly, he is a Republican, and although I am not a Democrat, but consider myself an Independent, I must admit that if I had to make a choice, it would be for people not money. Thus I would be for the Democratic Party.

I enjoy dining out, and the theatre. He is particular about what he eats, and he does not like many foods. After several tries with theatre going, I became tired of watching him sleep and now attend the theatre with friends or go alone. Our dining out must be in restaurants that serve American food. If I have the urge to eat ethnic, I go with friends.

We have remained this way for twenty-three years. In that time, my two children, who had been ten and fifteen when my husband and I divorced, became adults. In those years, we grew from middle-aged people to senior citizens. It became apparent that neither of us was leaving the other, despite the many differences between us. We were married in 2003 but have retained our separate residences, with my retirement in 2003 and my husband retiring in 2007.

Despite the many ways we are different, there are multiple positive factors in our staying together. We both like our space. Neither of us feels that we must have someone living with us at all times. It is nice to get away, to just be alone, to think and pursue whatever thoughts and interests there are just for oneself. Since our retirements, we have traveled extensively, and because my finances have improved, I am able to pay for half of our trips.

Having been born in Chicago, I am no stranger to cold, unpleasant, snowy weather. However, I noticed an interesting thing. Contending with and fighting the savage winters did not seem to come more easily the more I endured them. Rather, it was the opposite. While I was still working, I stated that when I retired, I wished to spend winters in a warm climate. Because I have friends in Florida, that seemed to be a good destination. We were not able to purchase a condominium because I would have had to pay for all the upkeep, and despite an improved financial condition, I was still not able to do so. As a compromise, my husband has paid for me to winter in Florida for the past nine years, and I am ever grateful for this. He comes and goes, as he rightfully fears leaving our residences in a cold northern climate.

There are other reasons for me to be grateful. Because he is an engineer who is both knowledgeable and handy with almost everything in a home, he helps me with household projects at every turn. He does this willingly, even eagerly, but nevertheless feels that all of his work is not important to me. Nothing could be further from the truth. I value and appreciate all the help and assistance he has given me over the years and the fact that he continues to give it freely.

I have spent much time talking about our differences. There are many similarities that draw us together, the major one being that over the past thirty plus years, we have managed to live with and overcome those differences. We love each other, and our mutual love and respect draw us together. He has helped me so much, and I believe that I have enriched his life with family, friends and a togetherness that we both share and believe in. For us, separate but together works in a wonderful way!

# The Stories of David and Kim

David Cole and Kim Griffin

## David's Story

When my wife passed away in 2011, my world of happiness, of loving companionship and of a predictable future abruptly terminated.

The following weeks were filled with periods of loneliness, denial, and a constant search to fill an excruciating void. Against all professional advice, I sought someone to relieve the heartbreak. After communicating with a number of women, one wonderful person, Kim, entered my life.

I was stunned by how much the world of relationships had drastically changed over the last twenty-five years. A predominant feature in my perception of this change was that women were prepared to enter into a relationship, but only on the premise that they maintained their independent lifestyle and place of residence. Suddenly, my idea of marriage, wherein the elements of love, trust, faith, and unity were tantamount, was shattered. My need for a relationship, however, superseded the time required to heal from a tragic loss.

Kim's courage and attempts to help me heal were undertaken at the expense of her own independence and her own desires to develop and realize her goals and dreams. This strain created a bumpy road for us to the point that Kim felt she had to sever the relationship. After three weeks of no communication, at an agreed time and place, we met for a coffee. Both of us had seemed to suffer the same distress and feeling of loss for each other during the intervening time apart.

It was at this point that I realized that denial had to be overcome, and in one excruciating day, I wrote a letter of dedication to my late wife. The following day, Kim and I went to the top of Mount Washington, and I read the dedication aloud. I cannot explain in words the relief I felt and the insurmountable weight that seemed to be lifted from my shoulders. The acceptance of loss was the key that opened the door to my future and the journey ahead.

Now I could concentrate on the kind of relationship that would be acceptable for both Kim and me. So many questions plagued me. Is it possible to endure a relationship that involved the two of us having separate residences and still respect each other's independence? Do only couples in a married relationship enjoy the element of trust? Am I compromising my faith by allowing this relationship to continue?

As it turns out, the issue of separate residences has unique advantages. At our age, either of us can invite and enjoy our families, children and grandchildren in the comfort of our own homes. We have the freedom to place our imprint on our own homes, forever identifying our own traits, character and emotions on the journey that each of us has undertaken. Why should we not feel the security within our own home, the freedom to choose the life we want to lead, and the opportunity to expand our individual goals and objectives?

One of the best dictionary interpretations of 'trust' is confident expectation. After having gone through a divorce earlier in my life with a first marriage, it is quite evident to me that this description is not perfect either in a married relationship or in the one that exists between Kim and me. In either case, the hurt resulting from a betrayal of trust can be just as horrendous; the only difference is the legal and binding contract formed in the marriage situation.

In our case, Kim and I suffered two different kinds of hurts. In my case, the death of my wife left me in a state of shock, loss, and sadness. In Kim's case, the hurt was one of betrayal, defamation of character, and abandonment. The time that it takes for the healing process to complete may vary considerably. Thankfully, with Kim's help, my healing concluded in a relatively short period of time, but then, I have been told that men do recover more quickly than women.

Friends and family were thankful that I had sought counselling. The men's group to which a professional referred me was not suitable for my kind of loss, and I abandoned this counselling after five visits. One-on-one counselling was far more beneficial because it isolated the emotions that were prevalent in my loss. The other benefit garnered was the awareness of how my emotions could impact my new relationship. The acceptance of my wife's death happened during this counselling, and I feel that a fourth session may be all that I need. I am well on my way along a different path and the journey that awaits me, whatever that may be.

My faith has certainly been a hurdle to overcome during the process of healing and within the relationship with Kim. Most of my adult life has been self-regulated by an urgency to give back to the community, to volunteer hours upon hours of time to organizations, whether they be sport or church related, non-profit groups, or community-based organizations. Oftentimes, these volunteer activities have been undertaken at the expense of family time and relationships. I began to question whether I had read too much into the quotation from Philippians 2:4 – '*Look not every man on his own things, but every man also on the things of others.*' Reading referenced self-improvement books and counselling further exasperated me; the underlying messages of 'looking after number 1', and 'loving oneself' conflicted with the values that irrevocably determined my relationship with family, friends and loved ones. A counselling session with my pastor helped to alleviate my conflicts.

The relationship with Kim further challenged my faith-based choice of life; after all, this is a relationship outside the institution of marriage. Pastoral guidance, although negative, will not thwart my objective of finding renewed happiness and of pursuing renewed adventures on my chosen path toward fulfillment and achievement in the years that lie before me.

As much as Kim and I have in common, there are marked differences that each of us endeavour to overcome. Whereas I enjoy a senior life in which I have achieved so much, Kim feels that she has been deprived of much of that opportunity. Kim has enjoyed international travel, whereas my experiences in that regard have been limited, and I have some degree of trepidation in undertaking any. I consider Kim a remarkable woman, and I have given her my heart unequivocally, but due to the nature of her hurt, it may be some time before she can reciprocate. Furthermore, if that were never to happen, I take solace in the fact that she has the courage and stamina to follow her dreams. I am so proud of her.

This LAT relationship that Kim and I have is not the easiest for me to accept. It is not easy to spend some evenings and nights alone, sometimes inundated with the thoughts of the greatest woman that was once in my life. It is not easy to embark on this new journey and to decide what adventures to undertake to add value to my life, thinking of only 'ME' as the benefactor. It is not easy to cope with this myriad of emotions that still grips me, even though I no longer wallow in the debilitating emotion of sadness. Also now, I frequently deal with new emotional challenges – each time that I leave Kim, I am confused for a number of hours over being 'apart', only to have these emotions supplanted by uncontrollable excitement over the thought of being 'together' at pre-arranged times in the future. I am sure that Kim, at times, has to deal to some degree with these same emotional stresses.

Above all, a LAT relationship offers each of us the unique advantage of freedom – a freedom to share solutions, but make decisions independently, a freedom to encourage and congratulate one another on a wealth of new adventures, a freedom to display and enjoy the affection for one another that suits the future we desire for each other.

## Kim's Story

Together but apart...are you crazy? Why would anyone want a relationship that tied her down without the "benefits" of cuddling every night, sharing meals and daily life with a partner?

When I first heard about a LAT relationship I was recently divorced after a thirty-seven year marriage, and I was wounded, fragile and lonely. The thought of a relationship where my partner would be miles away was unthinkable. Why bother? He would be having fun without me, living daily life without me, doing what? Could he be trusted? As for me, I would be alone and lonely waiting for our next rendezvous, without my freedom, and tied down by a "partner" who lived miles away. It was not what I wanted for this next new stage in my life.

So I thought.

Then, with time, more lonely days and nights, more healing, (and more online dating), I realized that in the end I have only myself to rely on. It hit me that I had to be happy and strong on my own, within myself before I could contribute to a relationship. What was I willing to sacrifice in my newfound freedom to have a relationship? Could I trust again? Could I love again? Did I want to be compromising and nurturing again? Could I live with anyone again? Did I want a partner? Time went on. I continued to grow and get stronger within myself and to feel comfortable with myself on my own.

Out of the blue, I met David (a widower), an online connection that seemed to click, and he flew out to meet me. Well this initial meeting was a disaster. He came on strong, showering me with compliments and gifts and scaring me to death. How could anyone declare love for another after only emailing and one meeting? I was a wreck, and after four days he left. I was convinced that we were not a match, but there was something warm, honest and likeable about this man even if we were so different. I also realized that we were also much alike. We were, however, and still are, at different stages of our grieving, and I was not the one to counsel him through his pain because everything was still much too fresh for me. David's pain was still very much on the surface, and this situation concerned me. We continued to correspond back and forth by email. He sent me flowers, chocolates and cards, and continued to edge his way into my battered and fragile heart with his kindness.

We now live fifty miles apart and have entered into a LAT relationship in that David has his home from his former marriage and I have bought my own place where I am working very hard to make my own home. I have a new community to break into, friends yet to meet, art contacts yet to make, festivals and activities that, with time, I fully plan to experience. It is a new and exciting world for me as I experience my new beginning.

Over the past year, David and I have settled into a relationship where honesty is paramount. David and I have had wonderful times together exploring new places and experiencing new things. We've travelled abroad together and enjoyed each other's hospitality. Eventually though, after being together for three or four days, I feel stifled, become uptight and feel a need for my house and time to myself. Why? I stayed with David for two weeks while I was looking for a place to buy, and it was grand. Why is it that when we are at my place or off somewhere, I feel smothered after a period of time? Maybe I need to work out sharing my life again.

David loves me and is very upfront about admitting to his feelings whereas I am not able to say those words to him. I love him as a friend. I enjoy our times together, but I am not ready for a more permanent relationship yet, or even sure whether or not I will ever be able to have one. My failed marriage left me with deep bruises and an uncertainty about ever giving my heart away again.

I have come to enjoy time on my own and almost need those alone times when I am responsible for nothing and to no one. As much as David is methodical, overly cautious and leery of all that "could" go wrong in life, I throw caution to the wind and relish the adventure ahead. Sometimes this difference in our personalities affects the outings we are on as I am aware of his nervousness and apprehension, but to his credit, he does push himself through. I see the other side of life. I aim to enjoy each day and opportunity and opt not to worry about things that may never happen. I need to experience what comes my way without explanation or guilt or even a lot of preparation. I need the freedom to do a U-turn "just because". I appreciate time to myself to read or paint, wander mindlessly on the beach or do nothing at all. I need my newfound space to continue to build a stronger me, where I rely on myself for happiness and fulfillment.

Yet, it is comforting to know that David is part of my life, and we do enjoy each other's company when we are together. He is very loving and accepting, but my intuition tells me that he is living in order to accommodate me and is somehow afraid of pissing me off lest I bid him adieu. If that is the case, it is not good. I have asked him outright about that possibility, and he claims it is not the case. I am still not convinced, but then David and I still have a lot to learn about each other.

I am not used to being catered to and showered with love and admiration, and such behaviour humbles me. Maybe that is the cause of my discomfort, as he sees something in me that I do not see in myself, and whatever that something is, it scares me. I need to be challenged those times when I am prickly, bitchy or out of line. I also love to be hugged when I am stressed and upset. I am not unfeeling. I have just become very protective of my heart. I love doing things for others, and David is so very loving and appreciative of my efforts. That response feels good.

I witnessed how caring this man can be on the occasion when we were driving to Edmonton to visit his and my kids and grandchildren when, on the second morning of travel, I received a call that my Dad was failing and that I should fly out at once. I had to get across the country as soon as possible if I were going to be with my Dad. I was rattled, but David stayed calm and pulled me through. He found me a flight, and then we backtracked hundreds of miles to an airport to get me on it and bade me farewell before he turned around, and for the third time, retraced the route. I was and continue to be so appreciative of his support for that effort since, because of him, I made it in time. I was with my Dad when he passed. David is so patient, a quality that I don't really have. I reach a frustration point much more quickly than he seems to.

Not so long ago, I asked David for some time and space, as I was concerned that things in our friendship were out of whack. The world felt as if it were closing in on me. I felt he was too serious about an "us", too dependent on me, and trying just too damn hard to please me. The circumstances felt very one-sided in that my goals and plans all of a sudden seemed to be his too. I felt he had not really dealt with his wife's unexpected passing, and that I was somehow a replacement for what he had lost in his life. Again, I could not be the counsellor, healer or substitute I felt he was looking for. I need my partner to be strong and confident within himself even if I am not. Wow – maybe I am asking or expecting too much?

During the weeks that we were apart, I felt a great aloneness and sadness, reactions that caught me off guard. They were somewhat unexpected, as I had asked for the break. I knew that David was a kind and loving man, and yet I was finding him needy, almost as though he were projecting his needs into my needs, and that perception made me feel anxious about having him in my life. I felt he had to heal himself to become a whole person ready to take on the world, and to risk a little to further his own healing and personal development before we could be a match. I did not like the thought that I would have to carry us both.

We met weeks later for coffee and our heartstrings tightened. We decided to try again. David had gone through some tough days of soul searching, questioning and reflecting. With the help of his pastor and a counsellor, he had come to realize that he had, in fact, been putting far too much pressure on me. He had come to understand that it was not fair to expect me to heal his wounds and that he needed to allow himself to grieve. The short separation and reconciliation have helped, but not solved everything between us.

We have agreed to take it one day at a time and to see where things take us. He has his home, his friends and his hobbies, and I have my art and other interests and "me" time.

LAT has become kind of like dating except that, instead of living at our parents' home, we each have our own. LAT allows us each to continue developing as individuals and to heal from our past. We arrange our visits/sleepovers depending on who is going to be where. When David comes here, he is very willing and skilled at doing those things around my house that I cannot figure out how to do myself, and of course, it is so nice to have an excuse to cook a meal and have a nice dinner and maybe watch a movie together.

Too often when I am on my own, I make do with much less so that it is nice to share those moments with a loving and appreciative partner again. I am not sure I have ever been the recipient of such adoration and support and, as stated earlier, it humbles me still. When I am at his home, I love working in his huge garden, his pride and joy. I hope that things balance out in that respect as LAT does tend to screw up our time to get things done at our own homes or even complete our own projects. We need to learn to take things along with us so we can do both things together, but also things apart.

I have to get over the feeling that David needs a woman in his life to feel complete. I need for him to admit openly that I am different from his late wife and that I can not be expected to be a substitute, but rather that I am a new and very different woman who has stumbled into his life at a new stage in both of our lives.

I was privileged to accompany David on a very cleansing ceremony for his loss where I witnessed his personal assertion of love and a final farewell that he wrote and dedicated to his late wife. He had come to realize that he was ready, and that it was time to let her go so that he could move on. He understood that he needed to do this for his own health and for the health of his family and friends. It was very hard for him to do this and very moving to witness, and yet, he did it so that he could move on. This event has changed David as now he does not appear as conflicted about seeing me. I feel it was truly a very powerful and real moment of honesty and sharing. My only hope is that David did it for David.

I need to get over the feeling that he is bending over backwards to accommodate my needs with seemingly little attention given to his own. We continue to talk about this issue and with time, I hope it will change. If it doesn't, this issue could be a deal breaker. Nothing would make me happier than for David to get deeply involved in something that gave him joy and occupied him in a positive way so that, when we did make time for one another, it was a sharing and exciting time. Physical contact, sex, and cuddling are all good. David showers me with compliments that embarrass me in their flattery, as I do not see those qualities in myself. He is growing on me and that scares me.

LAT is like seeing each other for the first time each time whenever we are together. That does keep those home fires burning, but hopefully with time, we can share some of those lazy days of a familiar relationship when one is reading, one cooking, one painting, one cutting the grass, whatever, but at the end of it all, we are together. Hopefully, it will come all in good time.

For now, for me at least, LAT offers the best of both worlds. We have the freedom to live each day as we need to, and yet we know that we have a faithful, loving, kind and good friend to share things with. We support each other through tough times and are cheerleaders for one another through life's challenges and stages. Personally,

LAT offers me my space and the comfort of knowing that someone out there loves and cares about me, for myself, with all my imperfections and idiosyncrasies. I cherish him as a friend, confidante and lover.

I cannot speak for David as I feel he would like more of a commitment, but for now this is enough. Our living and dating arrangement goes against his religious faith, and I hope it will not cause him undue turmoil, but that concern is his to sort out. We do not talk about his faith very often. I know it was a very big part of his life before he met me. That reality does concern me a bit.

The logistics of anything different than what we have now boggles me. I could not live in his house that he built with his late wife and my house is just that, MINE. Who knows what will happen in the future? For now we are taking it day by day, sharing, enjoying, talking, growing, cuddling and supporting one another. It is giving us time to think things through while knowing we are committed to one another as a couple. Our circumstances might never change, and yet things could change as I have encouraged David to jump at any opportunity where he feels another woman would love him and openly profess and show it. I still feel that he needs that kind of adoration in his life. I want a partner with whom I can walk hand in hand as equals. We are not there yet.

For now we are friends who love and respect one another in this new stage of our lives. For now it is enough.

# Love with Antonio

Kyle Laws

If I say that I chose this way, it would not be altogether true. What I can say is I chose someone who chose this way of living—together, but apart. Yet, as I don't believe in this sort of accident, what I can say is that I lacked the boldness to choose this way, and had to have it forced on me in a gentle way.

I am by nature a communal person: gathering people together for meals, outings, writing groups, sometimes wrapping all of those into one. For example, I organized a Dodge City weekend of poetry and art, participants sharing a bed and breakfast with a gourmet vegetarian cook in residence for meals. Some I convinced to come by train just as they might have on the Atchinson, Topeka, and Santa Fe when Dodge City was in its heyday. This kind of event is my idea of fun.

However, the man I've chosen to spend thirty-three years of my life with (so far) is by *his* nature a hermit. It is an unusual combination driven by the writing we share. Initially, the fascination was with someone so different from myself. I think I wanted to see if I was capable of being a hermit, or at least living alone, but I had in my mind that we would do it together. At least, that is what I must have had in mind when on Christmas break, I readied the rooms for him at the top of the stairs of the Victorian house I owned.

I steamed the red and gold flocked wallpaper off the large bedroom, a living room-to-be, with an iron (slow going, but it works if one is short on cash for equipment to rent), stripped years of paint from the brass hardware on the doors, pulled up old carpeting in the bathroom which had been constructed out of a closet with windows that pull in, not push out, to open. After a week of tearing out the old and putting in the new, I showed him the apartment I'd made for him.

He looked around at what I'd lovingly prepared and announced that he thought it too small. He knew what I had been up to when he left; and probably had spent the entire trip in a 1968 Triumph convertible driving through eastern Colorado and the Oklahoma panhandle, in the snow, rehearsing just what he could say in order to *not* move in. I remember being shocked, stunned, and finally angry at misjudging the situation so badly. I knew he was afraid of me, and my ways, but also that he'd fallen in love with me. How was this ever to work out? I am surprised, in retrospect, that the relationship of four months survived this pull by me, this push away by him. As frustrated as I was, I think I knew that he, and not I, was the cause of the impasse.

How I survived the ensuing years of pressure from friends and withstood the advice that I was being used as only a woman can be by a man, I don't know. Only after twenty years did people finally take for granted that I would live in my house and he in his—a small house I helped him find on the east side of town in what could be called the barrio. We were poor then and living as much by luck and timing, as resources available. To maintain two separate residences was a luxury few could afford. For years, I ran a rooming house while I finished college, not graduating until I was twenty-eight. He was never one of the boarders even though I had need of them to pay the bills. Also, while it is hard not to concentrate on his part in all this, I have known a combination of security and independence afforded to few. He has always been there if I needed him, and I've tried very hard not to need him. His fortunes have turned out better than mine. While I am much better off than those college years, I still worry about the future, but I don't want to be dependent on him. That independence – what he has shown me – has carried me through my whole life.

I didn't work for someone very long after graduating, but started my own business without really knowing how or if I'd survive. This move was an imperative driven by my own inability to take orders from people who I didn't think knew what they were doing, or if they did, they were acting out of fear, not from my faith in an independent way. This philosophy is what he gave me. In many ways, I have lived his life better than he would have, given my circumstances.

Since we're both poets, we have always had that art form to share. When we were younger, our days were taken up with the work we did outside of writing in order to support ourselves. This was long before the advent of the number of writing schools there are today. Most poets such as William Carlos Williams and Wallace Stevens had *day* jobs. We grew up with that expectation. That outside income also gave us more independence to write the way we wanted, for whom we wanted. We came of age as writers in the small press that was thriving in the 1980's, and we both made a big splash in our way. We wrote in ways different from the academics of the same era, and about different subjects. We championed our independence. Our relationship was in many ways part of that independence from convention.

In the evenings, we got together at a restaurant or bar (Pueblo being a steel mill town, there are many bars with good food), discussed the day and what we were working on creatively. I always saw us as if we were ex-patriots in Paris, only in a then down-on-its-luck mill town in the West.

These days there is less of the day that needs discussing so that the entire conversation is usually taken up with what writing project we're working on. I have since started a magazine and a press that publishes chapbooks. Antonio provides the covers for the magazine as he has dabbled in art since retiring from daytime work. What binds us together is writing and our mutual independence. And then there's always—wanting to go about life in a different way.

As I'm a poet by nature, I will close with this one written for Antonio, with whom I have shared thirty-three years:

## Love With A Poet

---

I fell in love with a poet
even though I was not one of those
who clamored around after he read
        and oohed and aahed
Disdaining those who did—
because I fell in love with the man
not the persona
But, it is the poet I cannot leave
This is something you can only know *after* 30 years
There's no way to know it before
How many mothers would it take to teach you?
That the poet can become his poem
That he can write it so many times
he becomes it
And while he says that he wants to go out
writing on the steering wheel of a car
as he goes over a cliff
                (A cliff he has twice gone over
                once with me in the passenger seat)
The cliff is not on a mountain pass
The cliff is *who* he once was
Free falling
Not into the sapling of a tree
        that caught us on the way down
But into the poem
The poem catches him
He does not exist separate from the poem
The poem has him—
the one after you write it
the one there on the page

something that is not you
something you don't recognize
something more than you could ever be
        without it

# A Roof Of One's Own – The Boundaries of Bi-Sexuality

Janette Ayachi

The notion of bisexuality has always existed in history; it has carried its binary baggage through myth, ritual, religion, literature and psychoanalysis whether it has been rejected, accepted or normalized. The issues linked to bisexuality can be just as problematic as the issues linked to homosexuality, but quite often the category is not taken as seriously.

The term 'bi-phobia' defines the discrimination and aversion against bisexuality, and 'bisexual erasure' disputes that it's often treated as a false sexuality, that it should be ignored or in extreme cases banished from existing on the sexual orientation scale. A common aphorism that supports this theory 'you must be gay, straight or lying' can be highly offensive to bisexuals.

So how far do the boundaries of bisexuality stretch and how hard or how often do they bounce back to slap us across the face? Can we really be bisexual and claim attractions to both sexes but settle with one gender in a committed monogamous relationship? Is bisexuality just a disguise or excuse for promiscuity or can we equally have just as many sexual partners being gay or straight?

I belong to the sometimes-troubled disposition of having labelled myself a lesbian in my late teens only to slip over to heterosexual-land in my early twenties when I fell in love with the least expected. That slip did not come without injury, so refrain from booing just yet. I am stereotypically categorised as a gay-until-graduation-and-slightly-thereafter class-A candidate.

In my defence, my relationships with women were not purely experimental. The purpose was significant; I was genuine about my feelings, and passionate about my sexual orientation. I suffered all the early secrecy of solo bedroom lock-ins playing Melissa Etheridge and Ani Di Franco on repeat, thumbing my copy of Jeanette Winterson's *Oranges Are Not The Only Fruit*, Radcliffe Hall's *The Well Of Loneliness* and all the other iconic classic coming-out novels. These were safely hidden alongside spine creased lesbian erotica short stories and Sapphic poetry anthologies.

I started my collection of lesbian-themed films and with that came a collective list of obsessive celeb girl-crushes. I always had a penchant for women in costume dramas so one can imagine my unadulterated pleasure in discovering Sarah Waters. I kept journals about my 'venetian tendencies' (using Daphne Du Maurier's secret code) just in case someone found them when describing Oscar Wilde's famously noted 'love that dare not speak its name'.

I experienced my first real girl-crush and consequent first kiss in the last year of high school, so when my time came to start university, I was ripe for the plucking and eager for experience. Suddenly I was free from any small town constraints; the world was my oyster and I was already wearing (or fingering) the pearls. I came out the closet, made my mother cry, dated what seemed like an endless list of fascinating women, fell in love with one of them and had a serious relationship that lasted almost two years.

I worked part-time in bars on the scene, wove my incestuous circle of LGB friends, wore baggy jeans, bandannas and eyeliner (which are no longer fashionable I notice), and was even deemed a 'lesbian pin-up' by onlookers. I drank Jack Daniels, smoked Camels, cheated a few hearts and got in a lot of trouble, thoroughly enjoying every minute of it – so where and why did the boundaries bend? When did my character slip from the L Word's bad-girl Shane to I-might-start-dating-men Tina? Well, there were a few men that I dabbled with, but never anything serious or even played out soberly. The men I can count on one hand, the women I need six hands to count.

So I graduated and began menial employment. Close friends dizzied off in different directions and one night on a vodka-soaked dance floor, I met a man who captured me instantly with his gaze. He asked for a light and I got a number in return. My mostly militant and activist LGB friends slowly pushed me off the grid, and I transitioned from les-femme party-girl to straight shacked-up couple-dom. We moved to the capital together; I started a Masters in Creative Writing and streamed all my ambiguous musings into a plethora of poetry and prose.

At the beginning, my friends mocked that I was a 'lesbian with a boyfriend' simply because my fondness for women never stopped although I was deeply in love with my boyfriend.

Almost two years forward into the relationship, I became pregnant and we had our first child, an event which distracted my urges, but I always eyed-up other mothers in the post-natal clinics.

In saying that my sexual identity was never in crisis, I just had to re-label myself as bisexual where I could safely desire both sexes from the side lines. I believe that bisexuality has a valid place in the continuum of human sexuality. A bisexual person can be just as monogamous as any gay or straight person can, and learning to legitimate desire without acting out on it is a challenge most monogamous relationships face. The boundaries of bisexuality are not rigid, they are fluid and elastic; there are no rules stating when and who one should desire and date.

Frankly, it should not be frowned upon by the bi-phobic crusades just because they strictly situate their sexual orientation on one side of the scale and choose to desire one gender type. Quite often bisexuals face the same prejudice and discrimination that homosexuals face, so why would we tolerate this preference just to define a 'phase' or join a fashion. I will not deny that there is greed involved, Woody Allen said that by being bisexual 'you are never short of a date on a Saturday night', but all that choice does cause conflict.

I do not look at men because I am with the man I have chosen, but women will always be aesthetically beautiful to look at, ideal to fantasise about and available to reminisce about fondly. There will always be girl-crushes, and I will always need the untouchable other of the same sex to inspire me. I call these women my 'pocket muses'.

I choose to be monogamous in the relationship that I cherish with the father of my children but, and here is the catch: we live under separate roofs. Co-habitation is hard, and a determinable amount of space for the self is so important. We have what you could call a 'long distance relationship in the same city', a few footsteps instead of a flight apart. In our relationship, we have sleepovers and all the appropriate wardrobe and toothbrush space in each apartment. The kids share two rooms and enjoy the adventure of living in two different spaces. I choose how I want to decorate the entire apartment. The masculine invasion of my feminine space is only temporary (i.e. dirty socks left on the floor, hairs all over the sink, toilet seat left up) and there is definitely less nagging and more looking forward to sex.

When we lived together there was always arguing... arguing about which way the dining room table should face, about whose turn it was to do the dishes, take out the rubbish, clean the drain in the shower...God! And it goes on... It was difficult to weigh up the housework chores when we were both taking turns working long hours, and then swap over and look after the children. There was even an incident where strict orders meant I could not buy another bookshelf for my expanding book collection because...wait for it...there was not enough space! I felt so restricted and so claustrophobic, and well, that as a human being I needed more breathable space. I was Van Gogh staring out from his asylum bars seeing spirals instead of stars.

Now, all that frustration ceases to exist. If I have dishes, I have dishes; if he has left ten scrambling pairs of socks on his bedroom floor, I no longer want to claw my own hair out of my head. We each have our individual spaces in which to flourish; yet, we grow together. How hard is it to dig oneself one's own cave in the side of a rock anyway? Two sets of bills just means equal pay in the relationship, and the cost is well worth having a roof of one's own to live, write, and buy more bookshelves in peace.

If something breaks our bond in the future, because let's face it, nothing lasts forever (except the strange longevity of chewing gum, but even that loses its flavour), well then, my inclinations would point me towards women again. We all have various ideas and standards towards habitation, sexual identity, and we are all entitled to the freedom to be able to voice them and follow our own lifestyle choices. As long as we are true to ourselves, happy with our own choices and honest in our commitments we can do no harm.

The conflict for bisexuals surfaces when, after all that bouncing back and forth desiring both sexes, we eventually have to settle down with one or the other (unless we are in a polygamous relationship that is). However, I truly believe that we *can* have everything that we want in life, just not all at the same time.

Currently, my family and our 'together, apart' living arrangement brings me immense joy and takes higher priority over fleeting fantasies about dark-eyed women in nineteenth century apparel, but the future is uncertain for everyone. It is true that sex commonly determinates the strength in a relationship, and good sex after bouts of no intimacy makes me fall in love all over again. This is more achievable if we have our own space, our own secrecy, and our own house rules.

In any language, simply looking at other sexually attractive human beings cannot translate into cheating; the definition of 'fantasy' is not 'to think about being unfaithful'. In being bisexual, we can make a choice to be with the gender we fall in love with, but we cannot choose to switch off all feelings and inclinations about the other gender we have maybe been in love with before. This perception does not mean that all our bisexual girlfriends are just with us until they meet the right man; it only means that when we are drooling over how hot Eliza Dushku looks in every single episode of *Dollhouse,* they will maybe agree but then comment on the cuteness of one of the male doctors in *Grey's Anatomy*.

More choice does mean more conflict, but then choice comes along with any sexual orientation. I was gay before I was bisexual, and I was far more promiscuous being gay. I am proof against the negative theory behind bisexuality, and I find it to be a very comfortable and accurate place to situate my sexual identity. Although I am 'together' with a man, the father of my children, I am very much 'apart' in the sense that I will always desire the other sex – this is more distance between us than space between our two separate roofs.

# Section Two
# Involuntary LAT

*"I love you and am wretched without you in our place."*

---

Some couples find themselves living apart but not by choice. The factors causing their separation are varied: illness within the family, the demands of a job, the need to retrain. The recent economic downturn has likely had an incalculable effect on the cohesion of families.

One heart-breaking story is that of Dianne Tchir and her partner who has Pick's Disease Dementia. Her thoughts are crystallized in poetry:

*you are silent now*
*as you hold my hand*
*I hear the shrill grate of your sorrow*

*we are not immortal, invincible or immune*
*one in six will be cursed with dementia ruin*

Although other couples have living apart together relationships for medical, financial or logistical reasons they don't necessarily accept living apart. For instance, Paul and his partner live on either side of an international border and, for a variety of logistical reasons, cannot see an early end to their LAT. They cope using a variety of innovative strategies and modern communication devices. Paul realizes the situation is second best, but the relationship is too important to sacrifice.

Daisy and Wilson live apart in an extended care facility because Daisy requires a different environment than Wilson does because she has Alzheimer's.

In another situation, Sara, along with her three children, must live apart from her partner, Jerry, who is a specialist in the U.S. Army. They cope with even more traumatizing issues than most couples as Jerry is frequently deployed to dangerous zones, and Sara must accept the risk of never seeing him again. She must also cope with Jerry's alcoholism as he self-medicates to cope with his Post Traumatic Stress Disorder. Her story is one of the most poignant in our collection.

Lastly, the story of Ian and Theresa shows that no situation is ever clear-cut. Sometimes one partner wants a LAT and the other doesn't, and other times, the preferences may switch. Flexibility and understanding are needed to work through such differences.

We suspect there are many more couples living in LATs who might have contributed were they not so anguished or stressed by their circumstances. Many, we suspect, are parted for economic reasons, for instance, needing to separate because jobs were lost but the house won't sell. Many are working two jobs and have little leisure time. Others are upgrading their skills and must relocate for long term retraining at a time in life where they expected to be building a future with their families intact. Returning to school unexpectedly late in life can be traumatising, especially when there is little emotional support from loved ones. Whatever the case, although Living Apart Together is becoming an accepted lifestyle for many couples all over the world, it is not necessarily a voluntary situation.

# Daisy Dear and Papa Bear – Together as Long as Possible

Linda Breault

I walk into the common room of the Creston Extended Care facility where I have arranged to meet Daisy and Wilson. During the past year while visiting my father, a resident at this care home, I have come to know Daisy, another resident, and her husband, Wilson. The two of them could be poster models for octogenarian love. I am deeply moved by the intimacy and commitment of their relationship and Wilson's vigilant readiness to do anything for Daisy. Their relationship has so moved me that I want to find out more.

Daisy is dressed in a light blue track suit, wisps of her long grey hair escape from her lengthy braids, and fuchsia-coloured nails match her lipstick. Tucked behind her ear, she has a freshly cut daisy from the bouquet that Wilson ensures is always in her room. In her late eighties, Daisy looks as if she were once a hellfire. I can imagine her as the 1946 Creston Valley Blossom Festival Queen.

Sitting next to her, his large hands holding hers, is Wilson. Daisy calls him Papa Bear. He is a towering six-foot, six-inches with a full head of white hair with hints of red from an earlier time. He's one year younger than Daisy. He's funny and smart and kind. Wilson always has a ready laugh and continuous smile; he's quick to find the funny side of things. That he adores Daisy is obvious. His eyes rarely leave her as he listens to her with his heart.

Watching how the two of them talk tells a story in itself. Daisy's memory is going now and she looks to Wilson to verify most things. He helps her find her train of thought when she gets confused and fills in some of the memory gaps. During the entire time of the interview, they hold hands and look fondly at each other.

They met fourteen years ago when they were both widowed, Daisy for the second time and Wilson the first. Wilson tells me the story of how they met and at the same time retells it to Daisy, whom he calls "Daisy Dear". Daisy adds to the telling of the story talking to him directly. They are having such a good time reminiscing about their first meeting, that I might as well not be here.

One day Wilson was in the bank all lined up for the teller when he saw this girl" come in who spotted him and marched up to him.

"You're Big Red, aren't you?" she asked.

Wilson agreed that that's what they call him.

She said, "I hear that you lost your wife."

They talked for a couple of minutes and, according to Wilson, her sympathetic response to him included an invitation to give her a shout if he ever wanted to chat. Daisy adds that she was kind of interested in this guy.

Wilson turns to her and tells her that she was just wandering around free and flirting with all the boys. When she hears this, Daisy just smiles.

Before leaving the bank, Wilson asked her for her telephone number. Turning to Daisy who is snuggled next to him, he reminds her of that first encounter, "Me not hearing very good, you yelled it out so you could hear it downtown."

For whatever reason, Wilson muses, he called her the next day and just like Daisy, she invited him up for tea. That was the beginning. They talked and talked and talked and started having lunches and dinners together. It didn't take them long to figure out that they saw eye to eye on everything. Everything just seemed right. They enjoyed their talking; they enjoyed their friends and their kids. Daisy would come roaring down his way and drop into the house. Daisy tells me she knew he was looking her way all the time.

Daisy says he was great company and she loved how tall he was. "I didn't want a short one," Daisy says. She checked him out pretty thoroughly and then decided this was the one she wanted.

"We just gelled on everything we done, didn't we, Daisy Dear?"

Both of them realized that being together was meant to be. Wilson tells me that it wasn't a teenage kind of thing with all that "I love you stuff"; it was just that they both knew they were meant to be together right from day one and he still believes that.

"It was a deep down kind of thing."

"It takes two to make a duet," Wilson says, "and we did." Six months later they got married.

Daisy decided it was too difficult to change her name once again. Wilson recalls, he told her, "As long as you are with me, I don't give a damn." They sold their respective houses and bought one they both liked, something that would be their very own.

They have a wonderful life. In fact, according to Wilson, their whole married life is like a honeymoon. "It was good the whole way," says Daisy Dear. "We are awfully lucky, aren't we, Papa Bear?"

They describe an ordinary life that for them is charged with a deep, abiding affection, caring and mutual respect for each other. They enjoy an attachment to each other that delights in the little everyday things they do together. It is never boring, never monotonous. They both like and love each other.

The last two years of their fourteen-year marriage have been different. Daisy had stopped doing her usual daily crossword puzzles and knitting. Wilson recognized that things were becoming more serious and sought medical help. Daisy was diagnosed with Alzheimer's disease.

Daisy had to receive more care than Wilson could handle on his own. He was able to get her into an extended care facility. They talked it over the best they could and decided to sell their house and have Wilson move into the assisted living section of the facility to be near Daisy Dear. He sees her three times a day; it's a must he says.

Once he had to go away for a few days. "It was difficult, and that hurt a little bit being away from each other," he says. They survived and Wilson suggests Daisy survived better than he did.

"And here we are, aren't we, Daisy Dear? I am happy being here and I am happy this girl is being looked after.

It makes us still together and we still have each other," he tells me. "I hope she is going to keep me around."

Daisy Dear teases him and tells Papa Bear it's a little late to get rid of him.

"We will keep on together as long as possible," says Wilson. "We will keep each other as long as we can."

And they do.

I leave deeply touched by their profound attachment to each other and how they have been able to live together despite the involuntary separation that has kept them apart only in terms of their living space.

Daisy died a few months after this interview.

# Poems and Commentary

Dianne M. Tchir

## Poems

---

Dianne M. Tchir

## AWARENESS~ The First Signs

I feed the woodstove
birch, spruce, and poplar
orange flames with blue
souls lick the logs
red coals spark
ending the glow
ashes left unattended
You overfeed the woodstove
Flames escape and
lick your fingers
burnt flesh fills the room
winter leaves me alone
mortified by the smell
of your flesh

## THE CURSE

I fit tight jeans
with my 49 year old body
that feels 25
kindles sexual desires
mocks youthful flirtation
seduced by music and your
piercing eyes that
cut the chains of
limitations and boundaries
get me out of me
I am coming to you
I drink liquid gold, flaming red
molten copper through
my third eye
I lick the cold thin icing
off the pond
your lips sear memories
steal my energy
your hands~arms pull me
close into your vortex
remind me now – the fall
of my life
your voice is brittle like glass
I go from bed to bed
not quite sure where to lay my head
you have become the bears you hunted
I lie in silence
arms flail, fists pound
with your roar, my tears flood
moans into fitful sleep

still I yearn your visceral
your thoughtful mind~you
you are silent now
as you hold my hand
I hear the shrill grate of your sorrow
we are not immortal, invincible or immune
one in six will be cursed with dementia ruin

## THE MORTAL COIL

We entwine meaningful moments
pay our dues to claim
bird, tree & sky

We live together &
apart forever
the very sight of you
means loss to me

Anticipation becomes
silent tears as you
hold my cheeks in
your strong hands
a kiss is locked in time
I love you...I love you
unable to let go

I cannot breathe as
I leave the echoes
of your room

# THE MAGIC CRAYON

You grasp the fat
green crayon
the wand

Hold it to the page
press down on
grass blades
as though colour
will magically fill
all the grass spaces

I place my hand on yours
with back and forth motion
you capture
the momentum

## ANGEL DUST

Still – frost clings to trees
brushing each branch & bud
with a stroke of Angel Dust

twittering jays, pine grosbeaks &
sweetie chickadees shake
the dust like a flurry
of sparkling diamonds

You strain to see as
you feed the birds

Dianne M. Tchir

## MISSING YOU

The mildew musty pine mixes
with evening dew
I crunch the leaves

The fall canopy is laced
with tears & I
lick the crystal pearl droplets

The moaning wind secretly
diffuses, steals slivers
of shivering shadows

Brown paper bag leaves
ride the thief that
meddles with night's dark secrets

I clutch the wreath of
freshly cut woven leaves
laced with your~my tears

## MY EROS~My Strength

In the misty mid region
I roam with my soul &
you EROS

my heart is volcanic
like the ocean gnashing against
rocks
wearing your sculpture down

Clock dials the morning
shadows lift at the end of the path
and a crescent spews ether
sedating our tears

I lift my finger bid you
trust me
kiss me
don't turn to dust
change the doom of this reality

things get washed and reused
except for deep scars
that discolour and taint
the tissues of life

Dianne M. Tchir

## SLEEP PASSION

My soul weak in deep sleep
I hear you feel you but
only darkness

I peer deep into this darkness
your glassy eyes stare back
shatter the silence

I whisper and you echo
murmuring back
stuck on my word

the wind howls through
the trees bending branches
scratching panes moaning
open...open

I creep with soul in hand
blinded by darkness

your glass eyes reflect
memories of us
I long and thirst for passion again
that river that quenches all thirst &
renews the fountain of youth

you mutter~I guess syllables/sounds but
your blank eyes stare and burn

my ablated heart
what prophet – thing of evil – temptress
took you from me
left you desolate unarmed
no words or sign of parting

your form fades
you hold me tightly but
leave me to my loneliness
and my lamp lit words
written with my tears

your pallid bust still flirts
streaming shadows in my dreams
this malady called living
will conquer you soon

my heart sickens with pitiful pain
at times I feel
you torture my brain
with this slow death

my bed narrows
now I sleep on
your side
night write words
that swell from the mattress
lull my body and
bathe me gently in dreams

to sleep only to sleep
as darkness dims the light
in my brain

## STRENGTH RISES OUT OF ASHES

The rain has ceased for now
saturated fields flood and
tear-filled rivers cry~acid rain
Sunshine soothes my worn spirit
warming my traumatized body
transposing me to another place & time
rescuing me from hot smoky coals
that burn my eyes; arrest my breath
uncontrollable wildfire that storms
scorching my mind's eye
All that I was is all that is gone
books and boxes – lost to me
except in my heart and memory
all that I am and can become
is held securely deep within me
Relics of saints, statue ofVirgin
metal crucifix from Grandmother's coffin
scapulas given by spirits past
Mother's and Father's urns – ashes
the holy rosary – beads of prayers
strung together
religious symbols I've carried a lifetime
And
**OUR FATHER WHERE ART THOU**
I tried to bargain with you Lord
praying with all the religious in my house
save it and rooms I promise to give
to those less fortunate than me
BUT
All was consumed by Baptism of Fire

Images of family, friends and me
lost their places ~ now walls of ashes
My pet dove~ the symbol of Peace
Given by my son was cremated
My oldest granddaughter's baby blonde locks
and the first tooth she lost
so many word strings and art by my babes and grandchil-
dren
sacrificed to appease the Fire Demon
Treasures and gifts for my children and grandchildren
and so many gifts given to me
Liquefied, melted, forged forever together
Amongst the smouldering ashes
**THE WINDMASTER TOOK YOU AWAY**
**FROM THE FLAMES**
**FROM ME**
Now my heart aches to see, touch & know
What's left of the man I treasure
Flesh hangs on to bone where muscle and strength
Used to be
A skeleton unable to walk side by side with me
And asks WHY?
Your gaunt face constricted
unable to smile
Dementia has taken its toll
you were moved three times
when the firestorm struck
and now
your pale blue eyes stare sharply
pleading for mercy , it seems
but
When I ask if you want to go home
You squeeze my hand, crushing finger bones

once again I ask
how can I cheat death – your death ?
this god – my god
this time – our time
We have taken so much for granted
Breathing deeply as we walk through the forest
Smelling, tasting, chewing, swallowing
Thinking, speaking
Blinking, winking
Hugging, kissing, clapping
Wishing, hoping, dancing
Smiling and frowning.
Tears well up as you grimace
I know your feelings of sadness and pain
Please don't leave – remain
Be gone death
We have lost all material things
You turn your head to hear magpies
To see the wind – rustling the leaves
You hear voices you recognize
And now as you take your last
Deep breath into me
Your strength and knowing
Above all things-I have not lost
The people we cherish and
Your living Spirit will join Mother Nature
In healing my wounds

# Commentary

These poems were written during a time in our lives when we were together but apart because my partner was suffering from Pick's Disease Dementia.

## AWARENESS – The First Signs, page 125

What happened? You would never disrespect fire, and how was I to know fire would bring about our ultimate separation?

My awareness of change in you was burnt into my memory. You couldn't stop putting logs into the woodstove. The fire, though warming, burnt your fingers and the smell of your burning flesh filled my heart and mind as I led you away, wondering what would happen next.

Your balance problems, speech difficulty, as well as your lack of understanding and empathy invaded your being. I cared for you and took a course about dementia after you were diagnosed. How could this happen to my partner: we had found each other in the Fall of our lives and knew that love was wasted on the young. We had the same interests: hunting, fishing, canoeing, and my poetry.

Caring for you became difficult. Although a simple routine of activities such as math, exercising, crafts and puzzles held your interest for a while, you slipped further inside. You no longer listened to cues, so when you fell, you couldn't help to get your six-foot two-inch torso up again.

With everything that happened, it was decided that you would safer in a care facility. I signed involuntary separation papers and was left asking, "Why us?"

## THE CURSE, page 127

The curse was upon you and memories of life together flashed back as I drove to see you again and again. We had a strong connection with nature and each other. The horror of dementia brought out many trapped animals within you, and fear found me. You held my hand and I could feel your sorrow.

## THE MORTAL COIL, page 129

Each time I visited, I recited how responsible we were to each other. My anticipation was that you would stay and our love would be stronger than this disease that would lead to death.

## THE MAGIC CRAYON, page 130

On another visit, I watched as you held a crayon, unable to make contact with the colouring page. It seemed you got stuck on repeating words over and over again and on the inability to connect one idea to another – like using the crayon to fill the page with colour. When I placed my hand on yours, together we moved the crayon back and forth. Once you got the momentum, you were able to do it on your own.

## ANGEL DUST, page 131

This time our visit took place outside. We sat on a bench, watching the birds as they flew from limb to limb and shook the snow off the tree branches. I commented about how the snow and sunlight made each flake sparkle like a diamond. Your eyes blankly stared as you silently fed the birds. I wanted to believe you saw the Angel Dust.

## MISSING YOU, page 132

Once again it was fall and I walked through the bush carrying your spirit within me. It seemed you were entwined with nature and I could always find you there.

## MY EROS – My Strength, page 133

I had difficulty sleeping and I was lost as your body was no longer next to mine. You were fading into nothingness, ashes that would become a deep scar within me.

## SLEEP PASSION, page 134

Sleep is still with you. Through the darkness, your blank, glassy stare beckons me to follow you. I utter "wait" and you repeat it – stuck on the word. You go deeper into memory, and I long for your touch, embrace as we cross over the bridge of youthful emancipation and rejuvenation of our kindred spirits. But, then your mumbling sounds bring me back to your blank stare, and I curse the demon that took you from me without any warning.

I am left with only these words written with my tears. It is so hard to accept this living/dying malady. I search for your body, and when on your side, the mattress swells and slowly lulls me as I night write into sleep.

## STRENGTH RISES OUT OF THE ASHES, page 137

Fire and wind swept through our town* . You were moved three times and I finally found out where you were. As I drove to see you, the scorched and burning smell remained in my vehicle and within me.

My treasures – our treasures – were lost to the uncontrollable firestorm, leaving me with only memories. But you – you would still be alive. When I arrived you looked at me puzzled and asked, "Why?"

You were a ghostly shadow and dementia had erased your smiling face. I stayed with you for one week. The hospital from home telephoned to say the repairs due to the fire were done and that I could bring you home. Squeezing my hand, you showed me that you wanted that. You could not be moved and you could not breathe on your own. Swallowing was no longer possible and they fed you with an IV.

As I watched over you, I realized the roaring fire in the woodstove that had burnt your flesh had foretold the end of our everything, both the materialistic and you, yourself. I whispered it was okay for you to leave now as I accepted your last breath into me. You will join me again in the forest, and Mother Nature will heal the earth and me.

*Editor's Note: in May 2011 at Slave Lake, Alberta

# Living Apart: Lifestyle Choice of the Army

Sara Barnard

Living unwillingly apart while staying committed to a monogamous relationship is complicated. Relationships in general are difficult, but living separately adds its own distinct layer of impediments. Living apart can have its high points, like the anticipation that comes with the countdown to seeing our beloved or having the bed all to ourselves. Other aspects, though, can be bad or even downright ugly.

Jerry and I have only been married going on three years, but it feels as though we have lived apart as much as we have together. Jerry was a specialist in the U.S. Army and had just returned from a fifteen-month deployment (the same deployment chronicled in the docu-drama "*Restrepo*") when we met in person.

A single mother of two young children, I was in nursing school attempting to attain my second bachelor's degree.

Jerry and I met on the same hot August day that he arrived in town on "post-deployment leave", or the vacation that soldiers receive after completing a deployment. We were inseparable the entire two weeks he was home, and I had never felt happier. Near the end of post-deployment leave, Jerry surprised me with an impromptu ring-shopping trip, and we became engaged just prior to his returning to his base in Italy. We had planned to marry when he came back for Christmas, but unable to wait, Jerry and I tied the knot one month later over the phone.

Over the course of our brief courtship, it came to light that we had attended the same high school only two years apart, worked in the same places more often than not, and somehow managed not to meet until I began working with his father, who didn't let the grass grow under his feet when it came to introducing us.

Upon arriving in Italy with my children, Jerry and I were inseparable once again. The four of us turned an Italian villa with a view of "The Three V's", Venice, Verona, and Vicenza, into our first home. We had adventures… stowaway Afghani scorpions, car wrecks, getting lost with no cell phone, sicknesses, food fights, pregnancy, and wonderful holidays with his army buddies. Jerry's army base was small and family-oriented, so I was even able to attend work with him when things were slow. We were rarely seen without one another…best friends in every sense of the word. If only the army had paid me for showing up, too!

After living in Italy for a few brief months, we received orders back to the United States, this time to Colorado. After being in Colorado for only a short while, a fact made evident by the stacks of unpacked boxes that seemed destined to remain that way, Jerry received orders, expedited this time, back to Afghanistan. He wasn't going back to the Korengal Valley, but instead to some place called the Zhari District on the opposite side of the country.

"Phew," we thought naively. Then we picked up the newspaper a few days later. Three soldiers from the unit Jerry was being ordered to fortify, who had been in the country only two months, had been killed by an Improvised Explosive Device, an IED. It seemed that the Zhari District wasn't going to be the "walk in the park" we'd hoped it would be.

Since our new baby was only six-weeks-old when Jerry was set to deploy, the children and I relocated to our hometown, a warm West Texas city far out in the desert and hundreds of miles from anything more military than a rogue recruiting office or decrepit Veterans of Foreign Wars (VFW) post.

This was our first separation in our young marriage, and living involuntarily apart was difficult for many reasons. I was technically a "single" parent again, only this time with three children: a newborn, a three-year-old, and a five-year-old. I had the help of my family and a wonderful support system, but even that didn't fill the void left by my absent spouse. Even more problematic was that the absent spouse was not simply working in another locale for awhile…he was living, working, and recreating in one of the most volatile places in the world at the time…for an entire year.

None of the news coming out of southern Afghanistan that was aired on our hometown newscast was good news, so I took to relying on Jerry's daily phone calls and our occasional video chats. There was also a blog being kept by an airman stationed at Jerry's base that I had stumbled upon for news of happenings in the region. I needed news that offered more breadth and depth than the standardized black and white print newspaper article ambiguously stating: "One U.S. service member killed by an Improvised Explosive Device while on patrol in southern Afghanistan".

I read those impersonal, vague words so often it seems they burned into my brain the same way a branding iron burns into the flesh of an unlucky cow. Every time I read these words, my precious Jerry was the one who was the victim...until I was placated by his phone call that would come in as soon as the phone lines were reopened from the "commo blackout". A "commo blackout", or communication blackout, meant that all forms of communication were shut down following a casualty until the family of the fallen has been notified. If the family were unable to be contacted for some reason, the commo blackout could last for days.

During this time, I found it increasingly difficult to sleep, so I loosed my creative being. I started my first novel, and an excerpt was published not long after I began the project. The title is *A Heart on Hold* because my heart at that time, and almost all the time now while Jerry is away, was and is on hold. I wrote after the children were asleep and, during the day, tried my hand at new things: sewing, baking, and going to church. My daughter and I won blue ribbons for our baking and crafts entered at an event in a nearby town. We looked forward to church on Sundays and went all out, joining a Methodist ministry. Late at night, while I was waiting for the call I prayed would come, I sewed jackets for my children for Christmas presents.

In addition to my inability to sleep, I think I also went a little crazy, not only from the sheer stress of the situation, but also because of a medical condition called Hashimoto's

Hypothyroidism. I had had the condition for years, but three pregnancies had killed my poor diseased thyroid all together. As the gland died, it went absolutely haywire. One day it would produce so much hormone that I would be stuck in the chair with one panic attack after another and a chest full of heart palpitations. The following week though, it would dip so low, I would be sluggish and depressed. In February 2010, the doctors thought it best to remove it completely and did so without much hesitation.

"Thank goodness the army puts family first," I told both my working parents when the question of who would watch my children during and after the procedure arose. I just had regurgitated the phrase because it had been shoved down my throat at every meeting, in every email, and with every "welcome" letter that bore the army insignia since Jerry and I had been married.

The list of reasons *why* Jerry was unable to come home for my surgery was long, ridiculous, and non-negotiable. Thank goodness, once again, for my loving support system.

Whether it was the malfunctioning thyroid interfering with my hormones or the fact that Jerry and I had vowed that whoever died first would contact the other as sort of a morbid goodbye, the day I was cleaning the kitchen in our little pink rental house and the blue glass Italian lamp seemed to jump clean off the top of the fridge to its demise, I was 99% convinced my husband had become a casualty of war.

I dashed to the computer and up popped before my very eyes *the words* verifying that in fact a member of the U.S. Coalition had just perished in southern Afghanistan. The word "hysteria" didn't begin to convey my condition until the phone rang a few hours later and it was in fact my Jerry, safe and sound on the other end. After that incident, Jerry invested a couple of hundred dollars for an international chip to put into his phone so we could call one another at any time. For a while we could even text until we got the bill.

Being able to call Jerry anytime that I had a bad dream or just needed to hear his voice helped to ease my anxiety somewhat. There was once I called and he must have tried to silence the phone, but instead he answered it. I listened for two hours to my precious Jerry in an intense firefight. I remember having to make a run to the store and walking through Wal-Mart with my cell phone pressed against my ear, listening to a battle that raged half a world away, a battle in which my beloved was a key player. As luck would have it, Jerry's phone battery died before the fight was over. The few hours I waited for him to call that day were torturous.

Once, I had agreed to be Jerry's wakeup call at our allotted time. It worked out perfectly because the time when he was getting up, I was usually going to bed. One can imagine my surprise when an Afghani man answered the call.

"Salaam Alaikum," he said, voice eerily empty.

I was so shocked, I didn't know whether to hang up or run to the computer and Google some Arabic words and attempt a conversation with the man. So in a flash of genius, I said, "How did you get this phone"?

"Hello." I could tell the man couldn't understand me and his blank voice both angered and terrified me simultaneously. Possible reasons for an Afghani man to answer my husband's cell phone were obvious...obvious and terrible. Had Jerry's base been overrun and had he been taken captive? Had he been killed in action and the Taliban fighters had looted his body?

"I said, HOW DID YOU GET THIS PHONE!" My tone was rising and if I had been able, I would have reached through the phone and tried to shake some English into that Afghani.

"Hello. Hello. Hello." Okay, now he was interrupting me. Also, he was speaking in a spooky, flat, monotone voice. That did it. After a particularly impressive string of potent curses, during which time I may have called both him and the fool laughing behind him, "bastard sons of a three-legged jackal", I hung up and immediately called the Rear Detachment Commander.

It was a Saturday night and the Rear-D Commander was clearly drunk when he answered my call. I gave him the rundown of what had happened and asked if there had been any news of a firefight with my husband's platoon or any reported casualties from the unit.

"Just keep calling. Your call will get routed through eventually," he slurred.

Jerry beeped in as I was talking to the Commander, wanting to know why I hadn't called on time as I'd promised.

Sheesh.

I remember a night when I actually got to sleep. It was after my thyroid had been removed as my voice was still low and scratchy from the surgery. My cell phone rang deep in the night, one long ring. The caller I.D. boasted an Afghani number. After several expensive attempts to call them back, the same bland recording kept reporting that the number was non-working and basically, that I was an idiot for even calling it in the first place.

I knew that Jerry was out on a three-day mission to a specific hill, and that he'd left his cell phone at his base.

My imagination wasted no time flying into overdrive. *Jerry's been killed,* I reasoned. *One of his buddies must've snuck a phone out before the commo blackout and tried to call me and warn me before the Casualty Notifications Officer could call or come by. But now the commo blackout had hit; that's why I can't call the number back.*

I was freaking myself out at warp speed as I dialed the operator for some much-needed assistance. The poor woman…I felt bad for her. She tried to help me, but I was so keyed up, and with my raspy voice, I knew she couldn't comprehend the *importance* of what was going on. So much for my good night's sleep!

When Jerry checked in after his three-day mission, I was quick to inquire about the mystery call I'd received in the middle of the night.

"Oh that. I didn't think it came through."

"You *knew* about that strange call? What was it all about?"

"Someone packed out an old satellite phone. Figured I'd call you to say hi, but it rang, like, ten times. So I hung up."

Stupid satellites.

★★★

The time came for Jerry's two-weeks of mid-tour leave, and we somehow managed to get assigned a time around Christmas. Oh, the thought of my husband being home for the holidays was too wonderful to risk, so I dared not think about it until that call came in Christmas morning.

"I'm leaving Dallas-Fort Worth International Airport, see you in forty-five minutes."

Whee!

So we got Jerry not only for Christmas Day, but New Year's as well!

My daughter and I rushed from the piles of presents we had been sorting to the airport. We rejoiced in counting down the minutes until he landed and sang Christmas carols to while away the time. Moments after the airplane landed, a few gaunt soldiers walked down the jet way toward us. I didn't recognize any as my Jerry. He had dropped a significant amount of weight, weight he didn't have to lose in the first place, and looked so unbelievably drained. Our daughter recognized him right off and feigned utter shock when I didn't.

"How could you *not* know Daddy?" Her tiny voice was as incredulous as a five-year-old's could be.

"Because he looks like walking dead," I wanted to say.

Christmas 2009 played out in our typical festive fashion, minus one thing: my husband's smile. Oh, Jerry would look happy enough if someone spoke to him. He'd act appreciative and laugh if he were handed a gift or a dessert, but more often than not his mind was still in Afghanistan with the men he hadn't wanted to leave in the first place, and it showed all over his handsome face.

The stress of being home weighed on Jerry much more than the stress of being in combat. It took only from Christmas Day to New Year's Eve for his deliriously happy, loving, doting family to drive him to a breaking point.

He started drinking on New Year's Eve before picking a royally stupid fight with me, called our marriage quits and walked out the door. I was furious at him for ruining one of my favorite holidays. I was angry, furious and utterly humiliated for my sake, my children's sake, and that of my family who had come over to share New Year's with us.

"I love you," the text read. It came in a little after 12:30 a.m. I closeted my anger and told him to come home so we could salvage what time we had left. He wasted quite a hefty sum on a cab ride home, blubbering, stumbling drunk. I put him to bed on the couch.

"I can't even sweep in the bed wif you?"

I think not. I still have my dignity, you know. They'll be no sweeping in my bed, thank you very much.

"I haf a headache, gonna take some of that headache medicine from Colorado. Where it at?"

I pointed him in the direction of the medicine cabinet. A moment later, he returned dutifully to his couch-bed.

"I don't feel too good. How many of those can I take?"

You know as well as I do you can only have one every twenty-four hours.

"Oh I took more dan that."

Seriously! What is with the drama? I could almost hear my closeted anger banging to be let out. Then his eyes started doing something funny.

Instead of taking the poorly-acted bait and freaking out, I said, "If you're going to overdose, have the common courtesy to go out and die in the front yard. You know the kids walk through here in the morning before I do, and I don't want them finding you dead on the first day of 2010."

As if on cue, he cut the act and followed me, trying once again to pick another fight, all the way to the bedroom. I conceded and held him all night. He finally cried himself to sleep around 4 a.m.

I didn't sleep…or sweep…that night. I stayed awake feeling very, very bad for everyone involved in the strange events that had transpired during the last evening of 2009.

***

I moved kids, dogs, lawnmower and everything else back to Colorado for his homecoming from Afghanistan, which, in the infinite wisdom of the Army, was slotted for 2 a.m. I found this timing very ironic since Jerry and his fellow soldiers had landed at the local airport hours earlier, just twenty miles away. Finally, our exhausted soldiers filed into the building aptly titled the "Special Events Center" a space where cranky kids proliferated. Then we were all were terrified by the sudden booming music of Lee Greenwood's "I'm Proud to Be an American," and the squawking zealot of an emcee.

I picked Jerry out of the sea of greens and tans in an instant. In an uncharacteristic stroke of luck, nobody came to shoo the children and me away from our outstanding spot on the floor, just off to the side of the soldiers' formation. Then, the much-anticipated words burst forth from the microphone, "Families, greet your soldier!" I was the first person onto the floor – after a mild encounter with a velvet rope barrier – with two kids by my side and one in a stroller.

Jerry met me in the middle; he had spotted us just as easily. A news camera filmed our first kiss in six months, as it had somehow managed to strategically place itself about one half inch from our faces. The lingering hurt from the New Year's Eve episode was long forgotten. Welcome home.

After leaving our mountain base, we trooped over to Denny's where we lasted all of about two minutes before deciding we were, in fact, too tired to eat. The kids already had the right idea; they had passed out in the booth. We had booked a suite to hold us over while we house hunted for our first house bought together. With the kids asleep in one part of the hotel room, the Denny's breakfast stowed in the mini-fridge for the morning, and us concealed behind a door in another part of the suite, Jerry and I weren't as tired as we thought. We didn't sleep at all until the sun was well into the morning sky.

I remember the feeling I had when I was finally able to hold him, the confidence in knowing my Jerry was safe. Nothing could hurt him, explode and leave him limbless or lifeless, anymore. War and death couldn't cause him any more pain, because I wouldn't let it. Everything would be okay; he'd survived and the hard part was over. Boy, was I wrong!

***

Sometimes separations within a relationship can be like an eye appointment where you didn't realize you were seeing badly until you were able to see clearly again. Living apart the second time may well have dilated the eyes of our marriage, and then provided a glaucoma diagnosis. It wasn't until our second "living-apart-together" separation that we were both able to see our twisted and tangled relationship through new eyes.

The second time we lived apart started hours after another of Jerry's epic episodes. Again, he turned to the bottle in tears over his Afghani experience and in reaction to a newfound, deep-seated resentment of me, and everything that I loved or even liked. Deep in the night, he kicked the children and me out of our new Oklahoma home. The tragedy of the situation was that most of my children were sick, and I had bronchitis. The E.R. doctor who was treating my oldest son for a dangerously high fever earlier that day had warned that my condition could turn to pneumonia if I weren't careful. The saddest part of all was that two of my three young children had strep throat and fevers ranging from 103 to 105 degrees Fahrenheit. The more he drank, the meaner and uglier he got, so he more or less kicked us out just as I was already packing the bags to leave.

Once he realized the kids and I had no intention of going back after we had packed up and moved as per his demand, a light inside him that had dimmed to black suddenly clicked back on, bringing into full light the man I had married. My golden Jerry had returned. He had hit rock bottom and succeeded in what he may have been subconsciously trying to do all along: push me away before I could push him away. It wasn't until that horrible, hurtful night that he began to receive the counseling services I beseeched of him. Moreover, he liked it, too.

***

Jerry was gone to a month-long army school when the kids, dogs, cats, and I grudgingly returned home to Oklahoma. After having been evicted from my home with my children in such a manner, I was more than a little iffy about when to return to Oklahoma, or even whether to return at all.

What I consider ugly is the fact that we even *had* to live apart the second time. Not because of military orders, but because of choices made, unfounded resentment and alcohol. This separation made him see our relationship through new eyes, as it did for me as well. I didn't like what I saw and he changed it. Perhaps we will be in a better place when he returns home, just as he promised.

And I will be here for him.
Like always.
Just as I promised.

# Miles Apart

Paul de Bruijn

When I first met Stacey, I know I could not and would not have told you that she would become my fiancée. Still, for all the miles that separate us too much of the time, here we stand, engaged to be married with one international border between us. I hate that distance. I hate the miles between us that mean that I can't just step in and fix things, even the things that I know I cannot fix even if the miles were not there. Yesterday would not be soon enough to bridge that gap. However, this isn't about the world we want to create, she and I; it is about the world we live in, and the good and bad of it all.

The hardest part of the long distance relationship has got to be the miles that keep us physically apart, and we cannot escape the fact that they are there. This distance defines the relationship in so many ways. When she is sick, I can't just go over there and nurse her and tend to her, nor can she do the same for me. We can't spend time just resting quietly in each other's arms as we want to. There is neither the touch nor the nearness of the loved one, and when an international border bridging that gap gets thrown in, the situation, becomes all that much harder. The legalities of moving become more complicated and drive home all the more the fact that there are miles between us.

Let's think of all the small things we do in a relationship when we live with someone, or near to that person and then remove those little chores from the relationship. Let's condense the amount of time we have in the same place to a few weeks per year. How do we put into words the importance of being able to do the simple household things together: preparing meals or doing the dishes as a unit as opposed to on our own, going to get the groceries and doing other shopping as it needs to be done? These times are hard to speak of because we all so rarely have those moments together, the ones that quietly build lives together and build a home.

When I asked her to marry me, the preamble was so very much about those moments. There was no ring; that came later. After she said yes, we washed the dishes together in my one-bedroom apartment, a scenario that might not seem all that romantic, but it was about building lives together, building a home through those very moments of shared household chores.

Still, not only do I not get to have these moments with my Stacey, I also have to miss moments with our children. I did not get to go to see my daughter graduate from high school, or see her off when she started college. I do not get to go to the awards ceremonies for my son. I want to be able to celebrate such moments with them, just as much as I want to wade in when things go poorly for them, but I can't. The same miles that separate me from my fiancée separate me from them as well.

We have become a family over the years. The children are part of my fiancée's life because she gave birth to them. They have become part of my life, starting from the fact that they were part of her life and now, because they also have relationships of their own with me. These connections have a direct impact on plans when I am there visiting. Not only does there need to be time for myself and Stacey to connect alone, but there also needs to be family time with all of us. I love both that romantic personal "couple" time and the time we have together as a family; neither amount of time is enough. I know that the children did not want me to leave when it came time to end my last visit there. I also know that they would have loved it if I could have come back with their mother after her last stay here, but that was not an option.

Those points of departure have to be some of the hardest moments, the ones when we go from having had the things we crave, to knowing that the next time will not be for a while, and all too often, for an undetermined length of time before we can have them again. The last time she left here, I stood and watched her for as long as I could. It did not matter that she did not look back; I needed to see her for as long as I could. Somehow, such moments encapsulate the whole. That which gives us the greatest joy also gives us the greatest sorrow.

There are reasons I asked her to marry me even though we live so very far apart. That circumstance was not a consideration in my asking. I asked because I want and need her as a part of my life. I asked because of all the conversations we have had over the years about pretty much everything under the sun. I asked because I love her madly, and she loves me. The reality is that the number of miles between us cannot change that.

As my relationship with my sweetheart changed over the years, I can honestly say distance was not a factor I considered, except for how it applied to practical realities such as living together. It was the relationship itself that mattered in terms of how it grew. I am passionate about both her and the relationship we are in. I look at where I am now and where I was when we first met and am so very glad of the change. Yes, I did the work because it was work only I could do, but she was there beside me along the way. There are more changes that I want to make, and I know she will be there beside me through those as well. It is things like this that keep me saying this relationship is what I want. And what I need.

As far as how I have changed goes, I would like to think that I have matured, that I have a better sense of who I am and why I sometimes respond as I do. I have become better in pulling back from that instant, heated reaction and getting to a place where I can deal with the situation constructively.

More fundamentally to our relationship, I have become better about touch even at its most basic, as in holding hands. This gesture becomes all the more important when I unthinkingly mess up on it and hurt my fiancée's feelings. It isn't just that touch is very important in a long distance relationship, but that touch is also very important to her. So when I pull my hand from hers without thinking about it, the act can come across as a pulling back away from her. Such was not my intent, but that is how she perceived the action all the same. Most of the time I try to be more aware of touch, to maintain the contact we both need in certain situations whereas in the past I would have disconnected without ever a thought.

When we are apart, we communicate almost every day one way or another, be it by texting or instant messaging or phoning or, more often than not, multiple forms all in the same day. That communication and the trust that it built is part of the bedrock of our relationship. We have talked about more or less everything under the sun at one point or another. In some ways, it may be how we have responded to the distance that separates us. In some ways it is also very much part of who we are. Talking and conversing just happens to be how we are able to share our lives, the good and the bad, with each other. This communication is how we support each other and how we grow together.

Also, there are the things we do to bridge the distance, for instance, the movies that we watch at the same time, or as close to the same time as we can. These synchronised actions are not the same as doing the same thing at the same place, but at least allow us to do things 'together'. The fact that I take an interest in what is happening in the lives of both of our children, and that I talk to them and want to do things with them also even if we are apart, are also factors that help to strengthen our bond.

However, we can never get away from the fact that there is the distance between us, and that in the end, all we do to build bridges across that gap are in some ways poor substitutes for what we would do if the miles were not there. Still, we keep doing them because the relationships we have built through doing so matter, and because they are ones that we want to keep building and keep healthy. This effort is really about a relationship that matters heart deep and more, even when the couple is separated by miles.

The distance can bury us if we let it. All the things that we cannot have can leave us worn out and weary because so much of how we express relationships is built around physical nearness such as, for instance, resting with our partner, just spending time curled up together and touching. There are a million, small things that one does in the course of a day when people live together. All of those depend on sharing the same space, on being near, and when we don't have that, when we know we want to have those moments but don't know when we will again, we crave them something fierce. We also pour all we can into the means of communication we do have. We try to find ways that we can do things together in spite of the miles.

I am so very glad for all that we have been able to discuss over the years. Some of the discussions were less than fun at the time. Some of them were very hard. Nevertheless, we had them, and we worked our way through those conversations as we had need. Moreover, we have done so much of it without the visual clues that go with most conversations. We had no choice. There were too many miles between us, and we have not always had access to webcams. Even those don't always work smoothly or give the full range of signals we would get if we were together in person.

In the end, what matters the most is that we are madly in love with each other and need to be together. It is why we keep fighting the miles that are between us and try to do things to make them feel less so for the moment. It is our commitment to each other that defines our relationship; it is the miles between us that keep us physically apart.

# It's Always Been Complicated

Linda Breault

Ian and Theresa agreed to meet with me in their little cabin overlooking Duck Lake. I drove the winding road along the east shore of the lake to the cottage that Ian has called home for fourteen years and in which Theresa stays when she is in Canada. Ian, a thirty-five year-old musician, sports well-manicured mahogany-coloured dreadlocks and has a quiet presence about him that is immediately calming. Before long, I was able to shed any biases regarding the distinctive Rastafarian hairstyle that often gives the "Rasta man" an unscrupulous and ferocious appearance. A few minutes with Ian would force most people to re-examine any negative assumptions that dreadlock-bearing men are unprincipled and barbarous. He reminded me of St. Francis de Sales and his thoughts about gentleness: "Nothing is so strong as gentleness. Nothing is as gentle as strength."

Theresa is a vivacious and loquacious twenty-eight year-old with sparkling eyes who bustled about the tiny kitchen to make me a delicious cappuccino, all the time telling me how she was so happy to be reunited with Ian after a long absence. She has a slight German accent from her native Dresden where she is now attending a nearby university. Theresa originally came to Canada for an adventure, first working as a Woofer and then as a nanny/ au pair. She didn't plan that the adventure would include falling in love and marrying.

I asked them to tell me the story of how they met.

## Ian

I was playing a gig at the Snoring Sasquatch on May 3, 2009. I have a thing for remembering dates! Before the show, I had met Theresa and thought she was pretty darned cute. At the jamboree later at a friend's house, Theresa came. I am pretty shy and fearful of the female species especially when I think they are adorable, but we talked a bit and I was seriously thinking of giving her my phone number, but before I could, she gave me hers. When she called me the next day, my heart was pumping. That evening, she came to the jam night at the pub and I watched her dancing. By the end of the evening I knew I wanted to kiss her and did. It was my turn to break the rules. That was the beginning....

## Theresa

> Ian was playing his washboard and his ukulele, and I noticed him watching me through the window. I checked him out and actually remember thinking he was quite cute. I used my birthday as an excuse and gave him my number to invite him to the barbeque. The next day I called him. I broke the three-day wait rule about dating.
>
> We met at the pub where Ian was playing and I danced. He kissed me on the cheek. I remember thinking that was too quick. I was really confused. Later that evening, we talked and talked until two in the morning. I was pretty interested in him but not totally smitten.

It only took Theresa a few dates to realize she rather liked this guy. The canoe rides and walks along the lake and to the secret waterfall only reinforced for Ian that he was totally enchanted by this woman. Twelve days later, they decided they were "together".

Within three months of being together, Theresa was offered a job in Canada and had to return to Germany to apply for a work permit if she were going to stay in Canada to extend her adventure. She wasn't completely sure how she felt about Ian. During this time, she was accepted at a university in Germany and had to decide whether she would stay in Germany or return to Canada. It was during this four-month period away from Ian that she realized that she had deep feelings for him. She decided to return to Canada and continue the relationship.

Ian believed she had made the decision to return to Canada because of the relationship and had felt lonely because of her absence. The separation brought them closer together and for Theresa especially, the time apart cleared her mind so that it was easy to come back and be with him. Through long Skyping sessions and telephoning, they began to find out how much they shared in common.

When Theresa returned with a two-year work permit, she worked weekdays in town and spent the weekends with Ian. A LAT way of living continued with shorter intervals apart.

Although it took Theresa longer to understand the depths of her feelings, she also realized that Ian wasn't the kind of guy who believed in marriage; he never wanted to get married.

## Theresa

---

It was funny because Ian had never wanted to get married, and I had always tried to talk about the idea, but he really didn't want to. For me there has always been a girl's dream of getting married. Still, if it hadn't happened, it would be okay. Being in love means wanting to spend as much time with that person, sharing the same dreams, being able to laugh, and fully trusting in each other. Getting married

> would have been nice. I gave up on the dream of getting married, but then Ian seemed to change his mind.

Ian who had never been in love like this before started to think that maybe marriage with Theresa would be how he wanted to live his life.

## Ian

> I never saw the point of getting married; I thought that in this day and age, people could love together and be together [without being married], but when you get to a certain point with the woman you are in love with…then there does come a point to marriage. I had never been there before.

Theresa had told Ian that she never wanted to live in Germany again, and that she wanted to make Canada her home. She had a goal of getting a university degree and started applying to Canadian universities. On February 25, 2010 while eating the Buddha's feast with fries at their favourite restaurant, he proposed. Theresa accepted immediately.

On May 5, 2010, they married exactly two years after their first date.

A few months later, they went to Germany and had a second wedding. It was during this three-week period when Ian was in Germany that he recognized how

Theresa missed her home country, family and language. She had been accepted at a German university to study a three-year program in Social Work. It was Theresa's understanding that they would be together but to live together wasn't necessary. She felt that simply the fact that she was married should not mean she had to give up her plans and individual life. Ian didn't want to force her into giving up her dreams. He didn't like the situation but did not put up any barriers to stop her. When they married, he didn't know she was going back to Germany for a three-year course, but he felt they could deal with the challenge and work it out. Red tape with Immigration Canada and entrance requirements at a Canadian university presented what seemed to be insurmountable barriers. With Ian's support, she decided to register for studies in Germany.

They went to the town where she would be attending university. Ian wanted to see where she would be living for the next three years before he returned to Canada. In the back of his mind he was wondering if he could live in Germany.

From August until February, they didn't see each other. They Skyped daily. Theresa was very occupied with university and Ian was working to save money to go over to | Germany.

## Ian

---

It sucked, but we knew it would be over eventually and that what we needed was patience to get through it. We are trying to

> find a way to make it work. We're figuring it out as we go along.

Six months later he returned for a visit. During these three months, he was assessing whether or not he could live in Germany. He wasn't sure. Theresa's course had only two years to go. They were creating ways to live apart together.

In September, Ian plans to move to Germany for a year, and then he wants to go to school for a two-year diploma during the last years of Theresa's studies.

## Theresa

---

> We would have to sacrifice everything to live together right now. Eventually we want to be together like a real family. We want kids. I could have chosen to let go of school but I wouldn't be happy.

They are looking at three options right now:

The first option involves Ian going to school in Europe at an English school to study horticulture (not available in Germany) during the last year of Theresa's studies. That would allow them to see more of each other and to be closer to Theresa's parents.

The second scenario has Ian going to school in Vancouver while Theresa completes her studies in Germany. The last plan is for Ian to improve his German language facility enough to study in Germany.

I asked both of them what they saw as their strengths in maintaining their relationship. Both listed trust, commitment, communication and being in tune with each other. They understand that living apart is going to be temporary for some time and know it's complicated, but also feel convinced they can do it.

# Section Three
# Trial LAT

*"I love you, but LAT just isn't going to work for us"*

---

Some couples have come to their new relationship aware of the pitfalls that dogged previous liaisons. Because they are doubtful of living together or are convinced that conventional marital arrangements are unworkable, they experiment with living apart together. Sometime during that trial LAT period, they realize that the arrangement isn't working, and that they, as a couple, either can't be together at all, or that they want to live together.

For Ron and Tina, the complication of orchestrating the needs of young children and ex-spouses delayed their decision to live together. Their story is fraught with the pain of several break-ups over the years as they tried to negotiate a workable lifestyle that satisfied everyone. Their experience, we suspect, is not unusual.

The epiphany happened for Ann and Ted in "Love in the Time of Swine Flu" when they began to plan how they would enact their dreams. Ted wanted to live out his long-time fantasy by living together; Ann wanted love but her own place, too. It just wasn't going to work.

In "Steve and Leila Try LAT...Sort of", Steve describes all the reasons that living apart is not going to work for the love of his life. Although Leila initially had well-reasoned misgivings about living together, she eventually agrees that there is more likelihood they will be happy together than not. Moreover, many of her concerns leftover from previous, unsuccessful relationships, have been satisfied in Steve's low-key, loving approach to her fears. For this couple, living together is their preferred choice.

The couples in this section all have in common that they tried a LAT, but couldn't make it work. Their stories may provide valuable insights for those who want to explore this new possibility themselves.

# Bridge to Love

Tina Lincer

The snow was falling furiously, blanketing roads and rooftops, when I left my writers' group to drive to my boyfriend's house, my typical Wednesday night routine. Three hours earlier, only flurries filled the night sky when I arrived at my weekly meeting in downtown Albany. Now, facing the whiteness, I was torn.

Turn around and head home, ordinarily a ten-minute ride? Or plunge ahead over narrow country roads to where my boyfriend lived? It was normally a half hour ride, though not tonight. The storm could only get worse, but my boyfriend was waiting, and I wanted to see him. It was our one weekday night to be together.

As I approached the intersection where I would either go left for home or proceed straight across the bridge over the Hudson River, I kept going – despite low visibility, unplowed roads and my fear of driving in bad weather. An hour later, shaken by the intense driving, I collapsed wordlessly into my boyfriend's arms like a silent movie damsel-in-distress.

When Ron and I met, on a blind date in 1997, I never could have guessed that he'd be someone for whom I'd cross a river in a raging snowstorm, or that one day, we'd be a bona fide couple: monogamous, loving, committed to each other. Nor did I ever imagine that we would live apart in separate houses – for ten years.

I didn't set out to structure my life this way. In my early 40's, as a divorced mother of two, I couldn't see marriage in my future. Ron and I knew that blending families wasn't for us. We'd each been married for more than twelve years and were equally squeamish about dating and long-term relationships. For me, dating at mid-life seemed like a cosmic joke – even more absurd and painful the second time around. Who had time for this? I had children to raise, bills to pay, and a job to go to every day.

Yet, I was too much of a people-person to declare that I preferred to be alone, without a life companion. So for the better part of a decade, Ron and I shuttled between houses, an imperfect ebb and flow of being together but apart. Call it dating, if you will. We bumped along, he with his growing kids in his small house on one side of the Hudson, and me with mine in my little rancher on the other side.

Perhaps it was symbolic that we had to cross a bridge to be together. We were constantly bridging gaps that kept us apart. One of our greatest commonalities, parenting young children, turned out to be our greatest complication. My children were twelve and eight; his, ten and six. Every other weekend, each of us took care of our kids. That left two weekends a month free. As fiercely protective single parents, we decided the most we could handle together would be dinner or a movie.

"Companionship, that's all," became our mantra.

Many dinners and movies later, though, we always seemed to be snuggling up in front of his fireplace or mine and going out with other couples. He and I became an authentic "we," at least while our kids were with their other parent.

The pace picked up. We spoke and e-mailed daily. Ron fixed the first of many broken things around my house, and I helped him move out of his rental cottage and into his new home. Then we had our first weekend away, in Montreal. Three days of laissez-faire togetherness and hot croissants in cozy bistros left us with an appetite for something more.

Soon enough, we started poking at the thing we did not want to call a relationship. We began to laugh at the ridiculousness of our "companionship-only" clause. We were officially a couple, all right: a couple of scaredy-cats. What did we want? Where would we like to settle/travel/retire some day? I wasn't sure about any of it, but Ron dreamed about living together in one house. For him, it came down to merge or diverge. Move in or move on. However, I couldn't envision taking four unalike kids, his sensitive country duo and my opinionated suburbanites, and throwing them together for better or worse in one house. It sounded like worse.

Not long afterward, discussing our situation on a cold December night during the holiday season when images and notions of family togetherness were everywhere, we cried, hugged and broke it off. I was bewildered and depressed. By then, we'd been together more than two years.

How could something so good go so wrong?

A few weeks later, Ron and I ushered in the millennium in different states but, missing each other, spoke briefly at the stroke of midnight. It was a new day, a new year, a whole new century. We got back together.

We agreed to do a few things with our kids, mostly barbecues or dinners; anything involving food seemed safe. Entire years passed like this, and for a long time, I believed we had the best of worlds, the perfect balance of togetherness and apartness. Others seemed to envy us, particularly married friends whose relationships seemed past the sparking point. The absence factor really did ratchet up the romance. Every time Ron walked through my door after I hadn't seen him in a week, I fell in love all over again.

The more in love I felt, the more I questioned the legitimacy of being a part-time couple. We'd go out, alone or with friends, then face the frustration and awkwardness of going home to separate houses. There were always good reasons – work, kids, appointments – why one or the other of us needed to wake up in his or her own space.

This "living-apart-together" business meant constantly negotiating and renegotiating our time and priorities. Not only did we need to sync up our own schedules and those of our respective children – job, school and community activities, religion classes, play dates, afterschool clubs and at least eight different sports – but also there were our two exes and *their* new mates' schedules to figure into the mix. It worked well when we were both on the same schedule, but any change, for any reason, wreaked havoc with our lives.

Living apart meant feeling like a teenager, always scheming about the next time we could see each other. Talking and flirting on the phone late at night were fine when my children were small, but when my daughter hit adolescence, I felt ridiculous and self-conscious. Sometimes when the phone rang, she would give me a rolled-eye look that said, "It's *him*." Then she and my son would clasp their hands together in mock pining, Little Rascals-style, and chant "how romantic." They got impatient when I stayed on the line too long, angry when they had to compete for my attention.

Living apart meant living a bifurcated life like my own children, between two worlds, two houses, two families, and learning very quickly that the thing one needs right away is always at the other house: shoes, briefcase, art supplies, favourite book or sweater.

Living apart, I worried we'd lose our emotional connection. There's some truth to the old axiom, "Out of sight, out of mind." Without having Ron around to talk to, listen to me or hug, I constantly questioned our relationship. Was it good enough? Satisfying enough? Would it last?

Still, living apart also gave me both the security of love and the freedom to be on my own several nights a week. After my kids were asleep, I could relax, write for hours, be completely silent or do whatever I felt like without asking or telling anyone. I cherished this private time, my secret luxury.

Meanwhile, Ron kept prodding me about the future, though he wasn't saying the "M" word, other than to restate he was never getting married again. Apparently, committing and combining families was no longer off-limits; he was willing to consider anything to end the untenable state of mid-life dating. When, exactly, he wanted to know, could we make our two households one and be a real couple?

In about ten more years, I thought.

I still couldn't see it. We had four kids in four different schools. Also, by then, both of our exes had moved in with their new partners and out of our respective school districts, leaving Ron and me custody of school residency requirements. This situation really rankled. The exes were free to go and do and live fully, but he and I remained stuck in an endless shuttle between two worlds.

The exes put themselves first, and we put our kids first, we told ourselves with a certain smug condescension. Were we right? Were we stalling? Were we crazy?

I was the writer who created stories and scenarios about our arrangement, trying to frame it in its best light. Ron, the social worker, analyzed and tried to problem-solve our relationship bumps and imperfections. Tensions built. Every time he packed up his clothes, his electric shaver and his briefcase and walked out my door, I was afraid it would be our last overnight.

We bumbled along like that for a few more years, breaking up and getting together again twice. By the time we passed the fabled, itchy seven-year-mark, we had commitment and history, trust and love, closeness and romance, but still no solid domestic agreement. Ron was on his third overnight bag.

"Rolaids, sleeping tablets, aspirin: this is the life of a fifty-year-old," he joked, holding up his toiletries case.

Then I hit fifty, and it hit me hard: In a few years, my daughter would graduate from college and my son from high school. Did I want to wake up alone and still be crossing a river to meet my man when I was sixty, seventy, or eighty?

In 2008, the year my youngest graduated high school, Ron moved in with me. Our children were already on their own or close to it. It was finally our time to be together. I was terrified. I'd gotten used to our odd little arrangement, even if it wasn't always smooth sailing.

Last summer, after ten years of living apart together, we passed the thirteen-year mark in our relationship, which means I have now been with Ron for longer than I was married. Even with children – all in their twenties now – in the mix less frequently, being together under one roof has taken some getting used to. These days, the challenge is how to negotiate our alone time. However slowly, the house that was all mine, a haven for me after my divorce, has become ours. I've made room for his things, including collections of antique clocks and vintage radios. His favorite club chair sits next to my antique desk, at which I pay our joint bills. We are no longer crossing the Hudson River late at night or early in the morning. We go to sleep and wake up together every day. Sometimes, friends, family members or total strangers ask, "Are you two ever getting married?" I guess we'll cross that bridge when we come to it. For now, being together is the lovely, most important thing.

# Love in the Time of Swine Flu

Ann Rourke

He found me on Facebook—Humble trucker seeks Pen pal.

Humble trucker? Pen pal? Ted, my high school sweetheart from nearly fifty years earlier had sent me this puzzling missive using his teenage moniker.

I was an ex-pat living and working in Egypt. My first response was negative. The message seemed flippant. I didn't know what to think. I responded, though. It was too tempting not to respond to my first love.

Thus began our three-year long romance between Cairo, Egypt and Vancouver, Canada.

Across the Western Desert of North Africa to the Pacific coast of British Columbia flew sizzling love notes from me:

"I ache to hold you." "We have a spiritual and emotional connection."

And back to me:

"I fall asleep thinking of you and I haven't seen half your clothes off yet." "I can't see anybody else in the world but you."

This was our love in the time of swine flu.

Sixty-odd year-olds acting out their adolescent dreams, we planned our holidays together, wrote daily emails and managed exotic phone calls from exotic places. "Sexting" became a new word in our vocabulary. My breaks from marking English papers were spent trying to connect on Skype. We believed a silver cord connected us. On nights of the full moon, I would gaze longingly from my balcony over the Nile knowing he would be doing the same, overlooking English Bay in Vancouver. We spoke as if there were not deserts, oceans, mountains and time zones between us. When we hung up and silence descended, I questioned what our relationship was about. He was my first love.

This high school sweetheart of mine had aged well. His leonine hair was now a thick mane of white curls; his tall athletic body was still muscular and lithe. He took my breath away. My mind told me to let him go, but my heart wouldn't let me.

On my trips home during the next two summers, we acted out our dreams. In the beginning, everything was love and surrender. He was an incredible lover. With me, he had the courage to ask me to show him my body, to ask what I liked. Like the besotted teens we had been, we lived out our fantasies. We hiked the Fife trail on Haida Gwaii, attended folk festivals in Kispiox, cycled the Pemberton pathways and canoed in the Tyax wilderness. Our quiet times were spent holding hands as we sat fireside or beachside, each reading our novels and sharing what we read. Our eyes often locked in recognition of the miracle of finding each other again after so many years.

When I returned the last year to work in Egypt, we both knew that our idyllic fantasies would have to shift towards what could be real. The school year and my teaching contract in Egypt during the year of quarantine from H1N1 were coming to an end, and I would soon be living back in Canada. It was time to make a decision about what our lives would look like.

At first, we planned the shared home. We would buy a house together near the ocean and live happily ever after. It didn't take long for doubts to creep in. While he dreamed of the love he so desperately wanted, I realized that a conventional relationship was not what I wanted. I had lived an independent and single lifestyle for too long to want to change. He wanted togetherness. I saw togetherness as smothering. When I made decisions, I made them without compromising with anyone or being compromised. When I cleaned the house, I cleaned my own mess. When I want to bed, I curled up with my latest novel without worrying about the lights disturbing another's sleep. Simply, I wanted my own space.

I also wanted this man in my bed. I loved being loved by him. He made my heart sing just looking at him. How could I not want to live with a man who had dreamt about one woman all his life? We played well together. I didn't want to give up our cycling trips, our mountain hikes, our explorations of ghost towns and old cemeteries. I wanted to keep wandering through art galleries with him and reading novels by the fire.

Why not keep the relationship as it was, I thought. The only difference would be a geographic one. I would have my own place; we would holiday together, see each other a few times during the week and live happily together but apart. His marriage had been an unhappy one, "living apart together" with the two of them sharing different floors in the house. I thought he would embrace this solution. He would have my love and devotion and his own space at the same time.

My high school sweetheart did not share my vision. He wanted more. He wanted the traditional marriage, the twenty-four-hour-day wife and the security of a commitment based on what he envisioned was a true relationship. Furthermore, not only did he want more, but he also refused to believe that I could love him and not want to live with him. This impasse was the crux of the situation. We could find no way to move forward. He felt betrayed by me. He was confused, scared, hurt and lonely.

Perhaps I had been naïve in thinking that we could have a loving yet unconventional lifelong LAT relationship. I thought it could work, but I didn't recognize his neediness. I fed his fantasy of being loved, a fantasy he had held for over forty-nine years. I had given him what he had been missing for so long in his life. How could I refuse this sweetheart of mine the resolution for which he so desperately yearned?

I did, though.

I miss him. I miss the sizzling emails, the plans for holidays together, the passionate phone calls, flowers, and poems. I miss being his pen pal lover, the woman he had fantasized about since he was a teenager, the woman who gave him a little bit of happiness in his sterile world. I miss his naked body next to mine.

It wasn't an easy decision to make. There are days when I feel guilty about being so selfish. There are days when I have to stop myself from contacting him and succumbing to his needs.

At sixty-five, I let my mind overrule the longings of my heart. I would remember the words from my favourite film, Casablanca—*"We will always have Paris"*.

I know in my heart that I made the right decision.

# Steve and Leila Try LAT...Sort of

Steve Miller and Leila Hunter

## Steve's Story

I used to get requests from women all the time to live with them because I'm good-looking and hot in bed. I had managed to stay single and enjoy myself until a foxy blond lady with great charm and intelligence stole my heart away, and made me reassess my plan about staying single and having several women friends.

I met Leila on an Internet dating site, and we arranged to meet at a coffee shop on a warm September day. I saw a tall, beautiful, well-dressed woman with swaying flaxen hair walking toward me as I sat at a table outside of the coffee shop. With her long blond hair, commanding presence and flowing robe, Leila looked like a lovely ship in full sail.

Leila saw me as a casual guy in a t-shirt, sandals and jeans and wasn't initially impressed. Still, we were attracted to each other right away; we laughed often and enjoyed an engaging conversation. I noticed her warm radiant smile, intelligence and contralto voice. In fact, I found this gal very intriguing and I wanted to get to know her. It turned out that she was the woman I had always dreamed of meeting.

After we got some good chemistry happening, I asked her over to my place for a drink and to listen to some good music. Things went well, and we sensed a good connection. She left for home with both of us wanting to see each other really soon.

We went on a few dates such as coffee followed by scenic walks, then a pub lunch, next a visit to Leila's condo where I admired her art collection. We discussed our interest in each other, and when she mentioned LAT, I said that was just another rock in the road that we could negotiate. Then we went, most memorably, to a lovely film about Glenn Gould. She couldn't help but notice how "excited" I was by her presence. The last date was magic; we had found that we were very comfortable and happy together, and we decided it was time to make love.

Oh yes, we made mad, passionate love all night in my cozy flat. Leila is a wonderful lover both in terms of romance and erotica. We couldn't get enough of each other! Over the next few months, we met each other's families and friends, fell in love and became soul mates.

Once we were in love and seeing each other often, it made so much sense to share our life together on a regular basis and live together. We've found that we are both affectionate, and very compatible in and out of the bedroom. We also share many interests. Living together has brought our combined interests, knowledge and skills to bear on life's issues and opportunities.

A year after starting cohabitation we are still strongly attracted, amazingly compatible, finding good solutions to occasional conflicts, having fun and enjoying the extended honeymoon. Believe me folks: living together works very well with the right partner!

So, looking at the situation from this perspective, I think relationships are dynamic and circumstances can change. People's thoughts about living alone can change. If both partners grow to love and trust each other and enjoy being together, they want to be together most of the time. They find themselves no longer dating others and spending more time as one. Soon they are living together most of the time discussing their future together, and one partner's home lies empty. They wonder why they're paying rent or mortgage when they're seldom there. Thus, some couples choose to move in together.

However there are a number of reasons why lovers may choose to live apart. Couples may not feel in love and just want a sexual relationship with occasional sleepovers. The relationship may be too new or uncertain for living together. Their work may be in different towns, too far to commute regularly. They may wish to secretly enjoy sex with others. They may find that seeing too much of the partner becomes tiresome. Children from a past marriage might make living together difficult. The couple may have been burnt before and don't wish to have their hearts broken again. People are afraid that a common-law relationship could mean lengthy litigation and may put their assets at risk, particularly without a cohabitation or prenuptial agreement.

Relationships are dynamic and the right solution for the partners can change. They should keep an open mind, as mutual love is rare and special. It is what people wish for. However, even though such love is amazing, it is prudent for both members of the couple to sign a prenuptial agreement before they live together.

## Leila's Story

After a rather chequered relationship history, including a nasty split following a seventeen-year marriage and several subsequent, failed romances, I decided to take a break from the dating scene to travel and work abroad. I was a mom whose children were now grown up and independently established; moreover, I was a mature professional well regarded in my field. I could retire, collect a pension and make a very attractive, additional salary overseas. It was a win-win scenario: make money, have an adventure and see the world.

Not a little of my determination came from anger. My last failed relationship had cost me plenty both financially and emotionally. I was starting to wise up: why risk the financial security I had managed to acquire in hopes of finding "Mr. Right"? Why continue to waste time and energy on prospects who increasingly seemed so wrong for me? Upon reflecting, I realized that I had been attracting men who needed to be looked after. Either they were substance dependent, emotionally immature or walking wounded. I decided I was better off to cut my losses and try a new tack: being single.

An extended period of celibacy wasn't necessarily in the plans when I took that flight to Asia, but in retrospect, it was exactly what I needed. The work I undertook was absorbing and rewarding. Before I knew it, I had been abroad for almost four years, had traveled all over Asia to Japan, through China, Tibet, Mongolia, Thailand, and the Philippines, and in the Middle East to Egypt, Jordan and Israel. Moreover, I had formed fast friendships with a wonderful group of independent, self-actualizing women. Interestingly, there were few men who interested me during those years.

Being tall, fair-skinned and strawberry blond, I had attracted attention wherever I went, especially in the more rural areas, but few of the men with whom I could conduct a conversation were likely mates; most Asian men regard middle-aged women past their childbearing years as matrons who shouldn't be interested in sex. Women such as myself are accorded great respect as "foreign experts" but, otherwise, we are seen as somehow neutral sexually. All of the Western men I met were either already married or interested only in doll-like Asian women. After a while, I quit looking, or even imagining that I would ever be interested again. Sexual pleasure for me became a matter of self-pleasuring. For quite a while, I thought I'd found my solution: be friends with men, but don't expect to find a life mate, let alone a soul mate.

However, circumstances changed when I returned home to Canada finally in 2010. In the intervening years, I had been back for holidays, but had spent that time visiting family and "couch surfing" at friends' places. There had been little opportunity to socialize on my own. I was ready to come home when I did. The last year had been punctuated with bouts of true homesickness for clean air and water, for uncrowded spaces, and yes, for interesting, single, Western men. I was ready to flirt with romance again.

This time, I thought, I'll improve my chances by checking out the Internet dating sites. I reasoned that my difficulties with partners in the past had come down to a few discreet, problematic variables, like age differences, lack of education, alcoholism, children still at home, or the interference of aged parents. I could control for those issues by stipulating preferences on my dating profile. Besides, I had decided that I shouldn't plan to live with a partner. I was convinced I would be better off enjoying an intimate relationship where we each maintained our own space and control over our own finances. I knew of other couples that had taken this route, and thought such a plan was plausible, if not foolproof.

In my profile, I called myself a "sensual, romantic spirit hoping to meet someone with a similar outlook". I also said one of my most important attributes was independence, that I could look after myself quite well, and that I wanted a similar quality in my partner. I didn't mention the LAT idea in the profile, but determined it would be high on the agenda of ideas to discuss at any first meeting. Finally, I said I was really looking for someone who still wanted to travel. I had seen much in my years abroad, but my appetite had been whetted to see even more. Besides, I had heard that one of the most interesting ways to manage a LAT relationship was to share regular vacations together. I really enjoyed traveling, but had discovered it was less enjoyable, and more dangerous, solo.

I remember spending a couple of months searching the profiles sent to me, and being dismayed by how few seemed likely matches. The key discriminators I decided would be education and the ability to communicate since, in every case, I felt past relationships had failed because we had lacked common interests or a shared ability to talk about them. Interestingly, very few profiles cropped up which included a level of education equivalent to mine until one day, while visiting a friend from my Asia travels, I happened upon Steve.

His profile attracted me right away: he enjoyed travel, he was on his own without live-in kids or parents, and he was a well-educated, retired professional. Up until that point, I hadn't contacted any of the matches suggested for me. Somehow, with the urging of my friend, I threw caution to the wind and sent a message suggesting Steve might like to meet me. Just for good measure, I sent a few other messages out as well, to matches that seemed less likely but perhaps possible. Then, as I was traveling out of town that week, I just put all thought of any matches aside.

Two or three days later, I was astonished by Steve's call on my cell. He too was out of town, coincidentally on a fishing trip in an area I knew well, having lived there during the early years of my marriage so many years before. Chatting about the beauty of that region up North and my memories of living there provided a comfortable context for our first conversation. I remember thinking that here was a person who didn't get easily tongue-tied, someone who understood the important social lubricant of casual chitchat. A promising beginning!

Back in town, we connected again and talked on the phone some more. I recall mentioning not wanting to live with someone, even though I had indicated an interest in a long-term relationship on my profile. His initial, somewhat puzzled response told me these would be murky waters to negotiate successfully. Either he couldn't imagine even talking about living together when we hadn't yet met in person, or he didn't understand how we could have any kind of "committed" relationship without living together. Still, I felt sure if we had enough going for us, that he might be willing to withhold judgment for a while. First,

I wanted to see if we could be friends. We decided on a coffee date.

On approaching him from a distance, my first impression was that he'd just got in from fishing! Casual dress would be an understatement here! I thought if he were trying to make an initial good impression that he might have dressed up a bit more, or at least not worn an old t-shirt. Still, he was relaxed, charming and articulate, attractiveness more resulting from an animated expression and startling blue eyes than from any etiquette book manners.

For the first time ever, we talked about previous relationships and what had gone wrong, and I heard some familiar refrains: not enough downtime together, too much emphasis on making a good impression, wasteful spending habits, materialistic greed, and ambition instead of intimacy. We shared some basic values that I hadn't anticipated! Still, I was wary of any quick decisions. I had, in the meantime, heard from two other Internet matches and had accepted coffee dates with them as well. Steve would have to be one of a group for now. I told him so, and he said he understood.

We ended up going to his place for a drink that evening. Thinking back, I can see what a risky step this was. In retrospect, I guess I must have instinctively felt comfortable enough not to worry that he would make any unwelcome moves. He didn't, unless a foot massage is considered inappropriate! Also, at one point he had casually caressed the small of my back as I was checking out some family photographs he had posted on his fridge. That caress, the first for me in almost five years, was electrifying! I realized that my libido was alive and well, that no matter how long I had been celibate, I wasn't past caring about finding that special someone.

We visited for about two hours, spending much of that time laughing at ourselves and the vicissitudes of life. We realized that we shared a similar sense of humour and several similar life experiences. We had both been raised as "Armed Forces brats" and had flirted with the counter culture in the 60's. We both loved nature and animals. All seemed quite promising when I left, knowing that I found him both intellectually and sexually appealing, but unsure whether he was the independent, low-maintenance kind of person I was looking for.

Our next date was a comedy of errors. We had entered the meeting place from different entrances and failed to connect for such a long time that I thought he had stood me up, and he thought the same of me. After we sorted that out, I followed him to another spot for lunch, and he took me down a "shortcut" that ended up at a dead-end in a cemetery. "How ominous is this!" I thought. When we finally sat down to order lunch, the construction crew on the road outside took up its work again after lunch break, with the result that all our conversation was conducted at full voice over the rat-a-tat-tat of the jackhammers. He looked genuinely crestfallen at the end of the lunch when I said I had to leave as I had another appointment (tea with an woman friend from my previous workplace). He had wanted to continue the date with a walk somewhere quiet and peaceful, out of the construction zone, but I insisted I couldn't stay. He thought he had blown it. I didn't say otherwise. Still, I had his cell number, and felt I could contact him again if I wanted to.

I didn't have to wait long to hear from him. He phoned again the next day to ask me to go for a walk. After the previous disaster, I must say I was impressed by his sense of self-confidence. I also reflected on the fact that he had dressed up a bit for the previous date, clearly realizing that I was somewhat attuned to personal grooming. I hadn't said anything, so I assumed he was showing some perception based on his checking out my casual, but always clean and tidy clothing. I thought, "Excellent! He's a quick learner!"

Our next date, a lovely walk along the city's picturesque waterfront, was mostly delightful. However, I wanted to talk about being "friends", whereas he said he regarded such a comment as code for "I don't find you physically attractive." I broached again the issue of developing a relationship where we kept our distance at first, and his reaction (I now realize in retrospect) was defensive, because he was sure I was seeing some other men I was meeting on line. In fact, I wasn't. I had decided to wait until I had got to know Steve a bit better first, feeling that other matches would be available if and when I chose. Still, his objection to "friendship" was worrisome. "How can we be lovers if we aren't friends?" I wanted to say. I had had too many flings where I had lusted after but not really liked the person. This time I wanted "simpatico": reality, and not just the appearance of mature love. I wanted substance in the relationship.

I decided to let a few days go by before seeing him again. I had agreed to attend some of the concerts at a weekend music festival with an old family friend whose daughter was in one of the bands. He was a person known to Steve as they were in the same business circles. I knew Steve thought it was a "date', and to tell the truth, I wasn't sure myself that it wasn't. The music over the weekend was amazing, but I found myself wishing Steve were there to enjoy it with me. In fact, I found myself thinking about him more often than I had expected. Clearly the "old friend" was not interested in me except as a casual acquaintance. Why hadn't I asked Steve to the festival? I was beginning to wonder what I was waiting for. Why wasn't I taking his interest seriously?

At the end of the weekend, the answer came to me. He was unlike anyone I had ever known. He was honest and uncomplicated in his approach. There was no manipulating or game playing, no posturing or hiding behind booze or previous bad history. What I saw was what I was going to get. He was an individual with distinctive, somewhat unusual tastes. I had never before met someone who liked fly-fishing, classical music and stamp collecting. What a combination! There was a kind of old world charm about him that was endearing, but I didn't know if I could handle him too much in my space. By that point, I had become used to living life my own way. If we were to become serious, he had to accept that I would retain my condo and he would keep his own apartment.

When next I saw Steve, we had decided on going to see a Glenn Gould biopic at the university. I hadn't seen him for several days, and was looking forward to the evening. The movie was engrossing; I was unprepared for how much I would enjoy the story or the music. At the end, we both left the theatre on a kind of high, exhilarated by the enjoyment of being together I guess, but also impassioned by the unfulfilled and lost love in Glenn Gould's life story. It seemed almost an object lesson. Why lose a chance at something promising? Wasn't meeting halfway possible? Surely two intelligent people could figure out some way to satisfy both their needs!

That night, I experienced a kind of lovemaking that I had never known before. Steve was and is a fabulously appreciative, sensitive and skilled lover. At such times, I truly feel as if I am alone in the universe with him, and that we are meant to be together. He, in fact, is sure we have met before and somehow got separated in another life. Even today, a couple of years later, we find ourselves thinking the same thoughts sometimes, and even completing each other's sentences. We marvel at the length of time it took to find each other, and revel in the years of adventure we have in front of us.

In the beginning though, living arrangements continued to be a sticking point. My one bedroom condo became our preferred "nest" so that Steve never seemed to spend much time at his place, to the point that, after a few months, he started to make noises about wasting the rent money spent on the place. In the meantime, I maintained that personal space would be an issue for me. I needed quiet to write and work on line. He liked to play music or watch TV sometimes when I needed the space to myself. He was retired and around the condo more often than not, so that I feared not only a loss of my independence, but also that he would become too dependent on my being there.

We had several spirited discussions about these concerns, his mostly focused on the foolishness of wasting money when we were both pensioners on limited incomes, and moreover, enjoyed being together so much, and mine on the practicalities of maintaining my own quiet space to work. We dreamed of finding a property with a studio in the back forty where I could hole up whenever I felt crowded; we even considered buying a duplex and splitting it between us.

However, we have had to wait for Steve's marital property to sell, a process that has ended up taking far longer than anyone envisioned. In the interim, we decided we could try to manage in a larger condo than what I had.

I refused to consider giving up my title to something. It would be my fallback solution should the relationship go south. Thus, we started looking for a larger place that I could buy: a two-bedroom condo with an office and two parking spaces as neither of us can manage easily without wheels. It was a hopeless search. Nothing was convenient or roomy or new enough. After several months we had to face the reality: living together would save us money so that, when Steve had the money for his half, we could afford a house with enough space to satisfy my needs. Then, I would rent my condo and keep it as a revenue property. The process of arriving at this decision seems so straightforward now that it's over, but there were times when certainly at least my temper flared and then in the aftermath, silence reigned. From time to time, I found myself wondering how it could work.

However, the beauty of this relationship is that I was able to broach these prickly issues without worrying that Steve would retreat into silence or become defensive. He is a remarkably easy-going kind of person, whereas I am a much more temperamental, but also a more practical person. More often than not, we have been able to talk the problem through and arrive at a workable compromise without either of us having to get upset. We are both direct; neither of us is given to guile. As a result, the gains made in understanding each other were incremental, based on honest realizations about what really mattered. I could overlook his failure to notice the little things, if he could forgive my occasional grouchiness.

In the end, we realized we wanted to spend our lives physically living together, not apart. I don't know how much of my initial reluctance was a matter of having been burnt so badly in my previous relationship, or a fear that this incredible man would move on if I didn't compromise. Somehow, I don't think the latter possibility would have happened, but he would have become more and more emotionally frustrated, and we would have lost valuable time, a commodity that, at our age, is certainly more valuable than money.

Today, we are still living literally packed into my small condo, waiting for the real estate market to settle down so that we can find a place with enough space to suit our needs: a master bedroom with two sinks in the ensuite bathroom, and an office for each of us. It must also have an outdoor deck and a garden, as Steve can't manage a sunny day stuck inside. We are agreed that if the door to my office is shut, he must knock, and sometimes I will not want to be disturbed. I must accept that he is happiest traipsing about outdoors, inspecting the landscape and watching for wildlife. I love to cook; he doesn't mind cleaning.

We compromise on what's necessary: I am a political junkie and can't miss the nightly news. He reserves the right to follow his favourite hockey team and watch any of their regular season and play-off games. I am a bit of a neat freak who can't stand clutter; he accepts my insistence on the bathmat back in place after a shower or the need to keep his stuff contained in baskets strategically placed in every room. He is a very security-minded person who gets anxious about unlocked doors, appliances left on and emergency brakes left off. I agree that I have a problem with these things sometimes. Our solution is to fine ourselves a dollar for each infraction, the money going into a pot labeled "Travel Fund". We are looking forward to using the proceeds on a lovely meal at some very posh restaurant in Europe next year, or on some other equally decadent delight!

While we are still mobile enough, we have a long-range plan of taking a major tour every other year. First, in 2013, is a three-month holiday in Italy, Spain and France with side trips to Austria, Germany and England if time and finances permit. Next, we are fulfilling a longstanding dream of Steve's to see East Africa, especially the Serengeti and the Ngorongoro Crater in Tanzania. Then, I want to take him back to Asia and show him the best of what I remember seeing there as well as catch up on whatever I missed the first time, especially Malaysia and Angkor Wat in Cambodia. Next is the South Pacific, including Fiji, New Zealand and Australia. South America and especially Argentina and Chile are definitely attractive as well; apparently, Steve says, the fly-fishing there is amazing! Our world tour schedule will keep us busy until we can't manage major independent trips any more. Then we'll check out the sea cruise options.

We have exciting plans that we both have made together, and we see life mostly eye to eye. Friends tell us if we, as a couple, can manage in this cramped space, we can manage anywhere. Apart from needing that physical space, what more could I ask? I am deliriously happy. I am far more content than I have ever been in a relationship, so that being "apart" for long periods of time is not desirable. I think some couples are just meant to be "together".

*Editor's Note: Steve and Leila have moved into a house with both their names on title, situated near extensive municipal parkland. The house has office space for two and a manageable garden where they both love to putter. During the last two years, they have travelled to Costa

Rica, Hawaii, Ontario, Montana, Wyoming, and Alberta. They are currently planning a six-week holiday in Europe. They continue to be deliriously happy.

# Section Four
# Miscellanea

*"Love comes in many wondrous guises."*

---

On first reading the following stories, one might wonder why they have been included. The criteria for the anthology are that the couple are in or have been in a long-term, committed loving relationship, but not living together under one roof. In the process of vetting these pieces for publication, we realized that both the terms "committed" and "loving relationship" were open to interpretation. A loving relationship need not be with a lover per se, but may be with a parent or parent figure. Commitment to a lifestyle choice may transcend one's feelings to an individual. One may feel some kind of commitment to preserving the fantasy of a former romance despite being married to another. Hence, we decided these stories deserved inclusion.

In this section we have LATs with a different kind of spin. First, the mother of a father and daughter separated before birth explores what it means to be blood-related. Another story explores a relationship lived in fantasy with a heartthrob from the teen years. Lastly, we have included a graphic narrative about a teenager's on-line gaming experience as an avatar, "Juliet". The attachment some young people feel for their on-line relationships in the gaming world seems worthy of being recognized as a kind of temporary commitment to a lifestyle choice, and a kind of practice period for real life.

Editing this section has made us stretch our understanding of the criteria. We think the results are worth the effort.

# The Secret

Joy Pritchard

There he was, standing in my daughter's living room, hands on hips, stepping one foot to the other. After nineteen years of silence, his first words were, "Why didn't you tell me you were pregnant?"

I'd been dreading this and here we were, about to deal with a decision I had made nineteen years earlier. I replied quietly but with confidence, conviction, and truth: "I didn't like you." Pretty brutal perhaps, I suppose he might have been expecting: *I wanted to go it alone, wanted to go back to Australia, wanted to be around family*. I didn't volunteer anything else and after a lingering silence he shrugged, "Well, that's one answer."

Flying around the Arctic on the Northwest Territories Government dime had been an adventure but also life changing for me. I was commissioned to do a feasibility study for the Department of Education – *Should we continue the Nursing Assistant Program?* It was important to me because I was the Clinical Instructor but all the students dropped before getting to clinical. So, in typical government fashion, let's do a feasibility study.

I was sick of flying – Twin Otters, Beechcraft, DC3, a helicopter, occasionally a 727. I was sick of the study, the idiotic questions without any real good answers, and the analysis to be done on my return to Yellowknife. I felt depressed, needed a hot bath, and *really* needed a drink. Lots! I was on the home stretch – Fort Smith today, then Tuktoyaktuk, Inuvik and home. So, to tie one on would be appropriate, medicinal even.

I dressed in my cleanest dirty pair of jeans, tucked into Mukluks, lumberjack shirt hanging out, layers underneath (January I think), toque, scarf, down hooded parka and wind-pants. Unglamorous but I didn't care. Just give me a drink. I don't remember the name of the bar but it reminded me of that scene in Star Wars – you know the one where Obi-Wan and Luke meet Han Solo: dim lights, smoke from strange pipes, odd characters belly-up at the bar, or plotting devious deeds in dark corners, and great music wafting from a curious band. In this case, it was twangy country music, and the odd characters were students from Adult Vocational Training Centre (AVTC). The smell was typical of most country bars – beer, cigarette smoke, horrible. The bleary-eyed bartender asked, "What'll it be?" I replied, "Gin and tonic tall, and keep them coming, please."

The man down the bar caught my eye. Not bad, I thought. Drink first, and flirt later. After a couple of tall ones, the fatigue of the day was replaced with happy, tired inebriation. Time to flirt. The man, also wearing his eyes at half-mast, held my gaze. I changed to beer. "What's your story?" I slurred as I slid down the bar, and he slurred back, "Tell me yours and I'll tell you mine." Until closing we swapped stories, lies probably…maybe. He was British, a cinematographer, working on a documentary in Fort Chipewyan, just over the border in Alberta. He described the treacherous ice road from Fort Chip, the only way to a drink.

So here we were: a girl from Down Under and a boy from England meeting in this strange setting. Later, under a northern winter sky, Aurora Borealis rippling green across the vastness, we felt no cold, just joyful, lustful, blissful intoxication. I slipped on the icy road and with his hand in mine, pulled him down on top of me into the deep snow, "My place or yours?" he asked.

"Mine." I replied.

During the night he whispered, "Marry me."

I whispered back, "Yes, of course."

Next morning, blushing awkwardly, we exchanged phone numbers quickly with promises to call. I rushed to the airport on my last trip: Inuvik then Tuktoyaktuk. Still in a fog, I thought, "A proposal, how about that!" Can't think about that now; put those thoughts in the 'later' basket and sleep. I had to be fresh and prepared for interviews with prominent leaders.

When all the interviews were done I called Tony. His lovely English voice on the answering machine reassured me he was real, but not there; he would still be in Fort Chipewyan. He wouldn't be home to Calgary for about a month, so I left a message welcoming him home and asked him to call when he got the message.

The flight from Tuktoyaktuk has lingered in my memory and it's difficult to explain or describe the beauty of the Arctic: white-on-white hinting blue, white mist curling off a frozen ocean, mingling with wispy white clouds swirling across a pale Arctic sky, no beginning or end, no top or bottom, but not whiteout. The drone of the Twin Otter seemed far away. Let this wonderful image remain forever.

When Tony arrived back in Calgary and my contract ended, he suddenly asked if I would come and live with him. After a long distance romance for a couple of months, we were willing to take our relationship the next step. By this time, I had forgotten what he looked like. Remember the night we met – dim lit bar, the Aurora glow and later in the dark hotel room, and our encounter through a bleary, boozy haze. I asked him to wear a pink shirt so I would find him in the airport.

His apartment was sparsely furnished but comfortable, with photographic and sound equipment everywhere. A huge map of the world was tacked to one wall with many coloured pins and dots. He could cook, but not my kind of food. I don't think it was Kosher, but it was high fibre. He was a health nut, except for the drinking. I don't know if his Jewish parents had influenced his life; he rarely spoke of them.

Tony had been born in Palestine before the end of the British Mandate. The family returned to England to register his birth and then had moved to South Africa. His dad was a civil engineer. He never talked about his two sisters, or mother, but just acknowledged their existence. Tony followed in his father's footsteps and, after his engineering degree, he moved to Kenya.

Do I believe the rest of his story, or even the beginning? Maybe, don't know. The only evidence to validate anything he told me was the 55 Magnum revolver living under his pillow and the world map with the coloured dots.

While building roads in Nairobi, Tony had befriended a young dentist and his family who lived on a little plantation just outside the city. He and Tony had gone to the city for groceries and on their return, found his wife and children butchered. The murders were blamed on Mau Mau rebels. This was too much for the dentist and he took his own life. Tony lost his mind and killed a bunch of people. The CIA lifted him out of Kenya. He became a CIA agent, yes, a spy, travelling to all the dots and pins on that world map. He was in Japan for a few years, and then Australia. He married an Aussie girl, but she divorced him soon after; she wanted a British Passport so she could work in the UK. He was heartbroken and never married again. This is what I remember. Someday, Tony's book will be published and then we'll know.

Living with this extraordinary man professing his love and wishing to marry me, I was miserable. This was not my life or the life I had envisioned for myself. I was also disenchanted with the phone calls he received from women all over the country and abroad – sexual, salacious, deviant even. He said he liked thin, beautiful women; I wasn't fat or ugly, just ordinary. I took long walks daily to get out of that pokey apartment. After six weeks, I'd had enough. I was bored, not working, and that's never good for me. Tony was working hard to find employment in the film industry, but immigration was a challenge. He was a wonderful photographer and able to get jobs in that freelance industry.

We took a trip through the Rocky Mountains to Jasper, he taking photos all the way. He had a fascination and a love of water, so every river, creek, waterfall, puddle, the Columbia Ice Fields, or a drop of water on a leaf, he took pictures. By this time, I had decided to leave but was keeping it to myself, vowing to tell him when we returned to Calgary. While in Jasper he approached marriage again, and I said I was still thinking. He was almost loveable, loving, thoughtful, even interested in my story, but he fell asleep. He was forty-seven and I, a pup of thirty-two.

Back in Calgary I got up the courage to say, "Tony, I have something to tell you, and I don't think you want to hear it, but you probably know it. I'm not happy, I need to work, I'm not in love with you, and your life is different from mine. I'll be leaving in the morning."

He said, "Okay." There were no questions, not even a "why?" just "Okay". It sounded a bit like relief to me. He took me to a lovely Japanese restaurant for supper, his favourite, and we had fun, laughed with the attentive waiter, and drank a lot of sake. We made love, and he fell immediately to sleep. I woke with a terrible sake hangover. I hurt all over, and the headache was horrible. Tony made sandwiches for the train trip to Kamloops while I packed. Tears welling, we looked hard into each other's eyes, saying, "Keep in touch," as the train pulled away.

I arrived at my brother's home that he shared with a couple of loud, funny men. He'd set up a space for me in the living room, and after hurried hellos, I went to bed.

A couple of weeks later, I thought I had a bladder infection so I went to the doctor. He came back and blurted, "You're pregnant." I was speechless. Irrational thoughts raced through my mind –*I'm thirty-two, too old to be pregnant. I'm not married. I'm a nurse, a midwife*. See, irrational, ridiculous!

The doctor asked, "What would you like to do about it?" *What?* I left the office so fast. I had to think. What *was* I going to do?

My brother was less than sympathetic, *"Idiot!"*

My family in Australia said, "Don't come home pregnant and not married."

Wow. And here I was on my way to becoming delighted, even when the nausea, in the evening, kicked in. Tony phoned a few times, asking "Are you sure you don't want this relationship? Because I do." I was close to telling him about the baby, but I didn't. If I didn't want a life with this man, why would I complicate this precious little person's life?

Finally, I said, "I'm going to Australia, I need a change and to get on with my life." I was anxious he might say he'd come too (oh no you won't!). Keeping the pregnancy secret, I was excited about the trajectory of my life, never thinking for one moment that I couldn't do this alone.

The usual trip to Australia would be Vancouver to Sydney, but who wants twenty-three hours of utter boredom and swollen legs? My trip would be Sydney ... via *Siberia!* I planned to visit my friend Heather in England and Merete and Costa in Denmark. I had missed Leningrad on a previous trip to Russia and really wanted to visit the Hermitage.

The train trip across Siberia was wonderful until near the end; catering ran out of propane to cook the food. Raw chicken is *never* good! I was arrested in Japan because I didn't have a visa (Canadians don't need a visa but Australians do). Hong Kong is a fascinating and beautiful part of the world. The week in Bali was delicious. Perth is probably my favourite city on the planet, and then Sydney. Home! Being nearly six months pregnant didn't complicate the travel at all.

A good portion of my money was spent getting to Australia, so I needed a job. I felt great and had no doubt I would get a nursing job. I was a registered nurse, midwife, and nurse practitioner; surely, there was something I could do. It soon became apparent I wouldn't get a job. Australia had unemployment benefits for pregnancy. I was mortified this was happening to me. Collecting unemployment was not something I would ever consider. I felt going on the dole was being a leech on society. However, I got over this impediment and was very grateful for the assistance.

I bought a caravan on time-payment; a sixteen by eight-foot home on wheels, very pretty, comfortable. I parked it in my younger sister's backyard. Julie was lovely; we became good fiends, and she took me to the hospital when Katie announced she was ready to arrive. Julie couldn't have any kids so this was as close as she would get to this wonderful experience. She cried, "We've got a little girl!!" We both cried. My heart was full, and I didn't even mind the 'we'.

My older sister, Pat, wanted me to stay with her for a while, and by now I had purchased a car (also on time-payment) and so bravely hooked up the caravan for the two hundred kilometre trip. It felt strange living like a gypsy in my hometown, but no one cared, least of all me. I was in love with my little daughter, and had a roof over our head. There was money in my pocket, not much, but enough. My unemployment ran out when Katie was one, and I *really* needed to get back to work.

Without any introduction, I marched up to my training hospital, Tamworth Base, asked for a job, and was hired on the spot! I was now one of two RN's in the Chest Clinic. Tuberculosis became my favourite disease from that time. People hate it when they are told they've been in contact with TB, but I'd say, "Hey, I'd rather have TB than cancer; we can cure TB but we can't cure cancer." After explaining the process and assuring them I'd be looking after them for the next year, they got over their angst.

My region, commonly known as New England, New South Wales ranges from Tamworth to Moree (a fringe of the outback), takes a small dip over the southern border of Queensland, east almost to the Gold Coast, and includes all towns on the lee side of the Great Dividing Range. The scope of my assignment meant I was away from home for four days every other week. It was horrible being away from Katie, but I had wonderful babysitters: Katie loved Penny and Ian. They couldn't have kids so Katie was the next best thing. I felt as if I had visiting rights when I got home on Thursdays.

This was our life until Katie turned two, and I realized I still hated the heat. I have fair skin, freckles and reddish hair. After I hit a kangaroo one dark rainy night, I decided we would return to Canada. It took a year to get passports and immigrant visas. Katie turned three on the flight, so the hostess took her to visit the captain in the cockpit. I had fleeting thoughts of Tony, but really he could be in England, or anywhere in the world. I kept it in the back of my mind that our paths could cross, but it was unlikely. I searched the Calgary directory and found no listing for him. See, no worries! I was doing pretty well by myself, and Katie was a beautiful, happy, delightful little girl.

Why must I always choose jobs that take me away from home? My new job in British Columbia was Nurse in Charge, Fort St. James Health Centre. The region, known as The Lakes District – Stewart, Takla, Trembleur and Babine Lakes, included three fly-in First Nations communities (Indian Reserves in those days) and three drive-to reserves.

The babysitters were a Vietnamese family who spoke little English. Lin, the husband, worked at the pulp mill and much of the time was laid off. They had two little girls and were grateful to have Katie for their kids to learn English, and for the money. Lin was a fabulous cook, and he frequently insisted we stay for supper, not just rice and stir fry, but a full five to seven-course meal, including shrimp! I offered money but he wouldn't hear of it, so I began buying books and clothes for the kids, and things for his wife, or whatever I saw they needed. When Lin and his family moved, I began taking Katie on trips with me. As much as possible, I co-ordinated my fly-in trips with other agencies – Drug and Alcohol Counsellor, Probations, RCMP, and one time a visiting student doctor. Katie fit in everywhere, with everyone.

The worst moment of my life was on a flight to Takla Landing. The plane had seats for six, including the pilot. I sat beside the pilot with Katie on my knee, probably not a legal arrangement. The smelly, slow, noisy, old Beechcraft droned along, and I was just drifting off when, *my door flew open*! I had a vision of Katie falling and of me not being able to reach her. I wrapped my arms around her tightly, so tightly she started to cry, and I shouted at the pilot, *"Shut the f---ing door!!"* He got out of his seat, climbed over the back of my seat while I leaned forward, crushing Katie even more, grabbed and slam the door. *Who's flying the plane?* I had that vision of her falling for years after. I never took her on a flight again. My thought at the time: Tony doesn't know he has a daughter so he wouldn't have to bear the loss.

The logging camps up at the lakes had closed so the train stopped running. The people of Takla Landing had no way to get to Fort St. James: boating was treacherous; flying was expensive and treacherous! The winter road was also terrible, and besides, most people didn't have vehicles. I suggested to Medical Services that three hundred Indian souls had no access to health care, and there should be a nursing station. They replied, "OK, you're it!" I agreed, so Katie and I packed up and moved up when the station was built. It was good because it provided work for the local people; it was bad because now there was money so more drugs and alcohol moved in.

Katie was in pre-school, and one day she came home crying, "All the other kids have a dad and I want one!" I told her she did have a dad but he just didn't live with us, but one day she would meet him. When the subject came up again I said, "Darling, if your dad was here you would have to sleep in *your* room, in *your* own bed." And that closed the subject for a couple more years.

There were many times when I felt guilt along with a kind of sadness, that Tony was missing the wonderful part of watching a child, his child, grow up. She was two, walking along the top of a six-foot paling fence, yelling, "Look at me Mommy, I'm very brave!" During a pre-school skating performance, I remember her stepping bravely onto the ice and immediately falling, getting up only to fall again, and again; they had forgotten to take off her skate guards. I rushed onto the ice, took off the guards and off she went, like an ice dancer. Also, I remember her packing an Inuit thirteen year-old dwarf on her back, in my plaid shirt, just as the Inuit women pack their babies. Thousands of moments like these I will never forget.

I was prompted to learn about education; I couldn't see us staying in Takla when Katie was ready for school. I thought of other women, the ones with husbands, who probably wouldn't *ever* think of going to college or university, or would have to consult, argue, compromise to do this outrageous thing. Katie and I discussed it (she was four!) and we agreed this move would be good. I wrote to Red Deer College and was accepted into the Bachelor of Education program. I was shocked and excited to be accepted as a mature student. Sometimes divine intervention allows miracles, and to date I'd had my share: I became a registered nurse, midwife, nurse practitioner, and now I was off to get a degree in education, having never been to high school!

Red Deer was terrific, Katie attended kindergarten at the college, and we had lunch together every day. No more babysitters! I completed two years successfully and it was time for sabbatical (no money for tuition). We went to Australia for a couple of months. On our return to Canada I went back to work in the Northwest Territories as a relief nurse for Lac La Martre, Pelly Bay and Coppermine.

It was 1986, the year Vancouver hosted Expo. I got a call from my friend Frank, the artist-consultant for that magnificent event. He needed to run away for a few days and wondered if I had a spare bed. Of course I did; I live in a nursing station! He and Katie became great friends, and I watched as she took charge of Frank: they built an igloo, rode on a Skidoo, and walked hand in hand over the snowy tundra to Bloody Falls. That guilty secret, denying Tony this pleasure, crept in again.

To top off the sabbatical, we took a road trip to Las Vegas, Disneyland, and Expo 86. We visited only the Northwest Territories pavilion. After the show, we sat on the Arctic rocks, munched on caribou burgers, and watched the other movie. Suddenly Katie cried, "Mom, it's me, it's me!" Frank had taken lots of photos of Katie and had said if he got them developed in time he'd put them in the show.

I decided to go to the University of Calgary to complete my education. There was still no listing for Tony, so no worries. Calgary was to host the 1988 Winter Olympics, so I felt how wonderful it was to be on hand for *two world events!* Katie was in Grade 3-4-5 and because we lived in student family housing, she went to University Elementary School. The school was chosen to participate in the opening ceremonies of the Olympic Games. Katie was in the yellow circle. When it was all over, Katie felt she had *opened* the Olympics!

I loved university, the professors, the courses, the colleagues, and our life. There wasn't much life outside of school and Katie, so the time went quickly. She learned to play the drums, modelled at John Casablanca, but gave up on the piano. I completed my degree by doing a six and three credit course in spring and the same in summer. It was done! I'd never recommend this; it killed my GPA.

The forecast was "no jobs for teachers" in 1989. You would think I'd be crushed; four years of my life, gone. Furthermore, I would *never* be an Elementary School Teacher. Too bad, I probably would have been good! So, I phoned my friend in Yellowknife and asked, "Where do you want me to work? Somewhere on the road would be good for me." I became the Nurse in Charge, Rae-Edso Health Centre, about a hundred kilometres north of Yellowknife, on the road. *Great!*

We finally left the Northwest Territories for good when Katie was going into junior high, in Edmonton. She was a normal teenager, learning about life, love, sex, friends, want, and work. She wanted a car so she had to earn it... and she did!

The guilt was still there, buried mostly. I imagined how different our life would have been had I married Tony: loveless, insecure in those early days, probably fearful...if his story was even real. Moreover, I suspect I would have been terrible dealing with marital conflict because there wasn't any in our life. Also, what kind of person would Katie be?

Katie was in Grade 12 and arrived home from school one day with, as she described him, 'an intriguing young man.' Shawn had long dark curly hair down to his waist, a goatee, moustache, long painted fingernails and earrings. He was a quiet, sombre, intriguing young man.

Once again, I was on the road with my job and Katie was by herself. She was fifteen; we've had "the talk". She was very responsible, managing two jobs, sometimes three and attending school. Still, a mother knows when her daughter is pregnant. I felt sad, guilty, and responsible. I asked if she had something she wanted to tell me. She shook her head. I asked, "Darling, are you pregnant?" She nodded and started to sob. I gathered her in my arms and said, "It'll be alright."

Jaeden was born October 8, 1996, a beautiful, healthy, nine pound, ten ounces! Shawn and Katie married when Jaeden was five months old. Soon after, Katie asked if I would help find her dad. I always said when she felt it was important to know her dad, we'd look for him. Amazingly, *I found him*! He was living in Toronto. She asked me to call, but I thought she should. She called, left a message asking him to call her. He called twenty minutes later, "I just received a message from a beautiful young woman asking me to call. Who *are* you?"

Katie replied, "You don't know me, but you knew my mother. You met in Fort Smith, Northwest Territories". He rambled for a bit, and remembered a woman he had met in a bar. She was doing some kind of study, and we lived together for a little while. After a long pause he asked,

"*Are you my child*?" Katie chuckled quietly and said, "Ah, yes I am!"

The secret was out – a relief but also a loss. The next couple of years were anguish for him; first denial, then disbelief, anger, frustration, hurt, hate perhaps, and sadness for the loss. This man, with whom I spent maybe two months of my life in physical contact, has been in my life every day. I see resemblance to her father in her facial features; she is beautiful, exotic, she is the mirror that reflects back to me this strange, unconventional union. Her hands are like his, and like her father she is a deep thinker, a searcher. When I see her smile, her happy countenance, her love of goodness, caring, and her spirituality, I see myself. I have never regretted my decision for a moment.

At the deepest psychic level I trusted my instincts, and I believe that living apart yet deeply connected was the right decision. Leaving her the choice to connect with him once she was an adult was also the right one. The second time Tony came to visit, primarily to have DNA testing to satisfy his lawyer that Katie was indeed his daughter, he said to me, "You did the right thing; your life would not have been good with me. You've raised a beautiful young woman, and I'm glad to know there is something of me in this world."

Tony and Katie have a long distance relationship and I think, at a distance, it is okay. Maybe knowing he has a daughter, and that they love each other in a distant kind of way, brings him some kind of happiness and joy into his life. I still don't like him. He'll just have to forgive me.

# The Fling I Never Had

## Phyllis Sweetwater

---

There was a moment in my childhood that stood out as a leap in my maturity. It started in Grade Five. Consuming my eleven year-old girl's mind and focus, where failure would have been the destruction of my terrified little heart, was one person; his name was Chris – Christopher Lamage. He had been held back a grade, so instead of joining his peers, he graced *us* with his presence, eager to share his vast knowledge and experience. We were his apprentices. He was a year older, a year less like a child, and a year closer to manhood than any of my peers.

Chris didn't have much to prove. He oozed with confidence on the outside, and if there were any secret fears hidden in the inside, I had no skills in finding them. He was so fashionable. He knew styles and music that were meant for teenagers. He was cool and everybody liked him. He never teased kids the way the other boys did; in fact, he was easy going with everyone, even the teachers. Being the geek that I was, I figured he was untouchable.

On a mild day the class went outside after lunch to goof around under relaxed supervision. I remember playing, "Honey if you love me" and making my first move. The idea of the game was to look the opponent in the eye and he or she says, "Honey if you love me, will you please give me a smile?" The point is to try as hard as possible very hardest to make the other laugh. The person asked the question had to reply while, at the same time, remaining expressionless, "Honey you know I love you, but I just can't smile."

"Phyllis, it's your turn." The teacher pointed at me. Chosen as the instigator, I picked whom I would victimize. Without thinking of the consequences of my assertive actions, I walked over to Chris and sat right on his lap. The only other male human being whose lap I had ever sat on was my father's. I was determined to open a new door in my personal relationships. I was done with girly, icky attitudes towards boys or trying to stay as far away from them as I could. I showed him my brave, new attitude and hoped his reaction didn't make me the biggest loser in Grade Five. Surprisingly, he didn't seem too shocked.

Next I flung my arms around his shoulder and curled my fingers through his long head-banger hair.

"Honey," I breathed in his ear, trying to impersonate Madonna or Cindi Lauper, "If you love me…" I paused trying to drop the hint, "Could you please, please give me a smile?" I pulled away a bit to show him my puppy-dog eyes.

"Honey," he replied, flashing his glorious brown eyes back at me. There was a small sign that he was about to crack. He pursed his lips, held his breath, but was able to blurt out, "You know I love you…" before he snorted a laugh and dumped me off his lap. I had won! Not just the game but also my self-imposed challenge. If the kids were snickering or gossiping I didn't notice. I had touched the untouchable, and that might be my only chance. The teacher later clarified that the rules stated no physical contact. I actually already had known that.

"Ha! It didn't count!" Chris bellowed, but I didn't care, even if he completely ignored me for the rest of the week.

The next week was different. I was utterly shocked when Chris asked for my phone number. He said he wanted to hang out sometime after school. This was a major move. I hardly hung out with anyone after school. Even though I wanted to so badly, I had no idea how to act.

When he called I ran into my parents' room (I didn't have a phone of my own) and locked the door so I wouldn't "get caught". I actually thought I was being disobedient. Being somehow "involved" with a boy was being as bad as I, in my prepubescent mind, could fathom. Chris admitted that he had a crush on me.

"But so does Peter." The conversation was full of long pauses. I figured he was being prompted.

"So what do you want me to do about it?"

Another long pause.

"Well, I don't want Peter to get hurt so we don't want you to choose between us."

The cryptic conversation went on for over an hour. He finally decided he wanted me to come over, or else hewanted to come to my house, but both options seemed too dangerous so we met at the park.

When I got to the park, Peter was with him. What was I going to do? What was his sidekick there for? Did he realize this messed up our chance at a first kiss? Being too afraid to come alone seemed out of character for Chris, but now that I think about it, he never did anything alone. He was always surrounded by people.

We walked up and down the path kicking rocks, looking at our feet. The meeting was frustratingly fruitless so we decided to go back to our houses and talk on the phone again. I was relieved, disappointed and extremely suspicious. All of that build up for nothing!

Sure enough, the next day at school, both Chris and Peter were very distant, to the point I was sure they thought I was a ghost. I figured they had made everything up just for kicks. They couldn't actually be seen in public with me because I was such a nerd. Whatever the case, it made me realize I was too young for such suspense and scandal. That was the end of that.

That first daring action set a precedent for the way I treated all of my relationships. I never sat on my dad's lap again – that's for sure. My many ex-boyfriends can all testify that I was an instigator and a tease. I went for the easy targets, so I thought I was justified in treating them poorly. I never had control of my raging hormones and many times, my flings would end in disaster. I played the dominant, pant-wearing female who committed to nothing.

Eventually, I got pinned down and married. I lost my 'active' lifestyle to provide my husband and two kids with a secure and nurturing wife and mother. Underneath the façade, I was anything but.

"Jeff, you make me feel like I'm in prison!"

Our fighting was getting worse. I was pulling away while my husband was tightening the chains.

"This is your life. This is the role you chose to play. It is your responsibility!"

"I think we rushed into this. We weren't thinking straight. We weren't ready. I am not ready."

"You think choosing me was a bad decision? What about having kids? Was that a mistake too?" Jeff, spoke with his hands. They were in my face.

"I'm not ready to resign myself to a boring life with a ten o'clock curfew! If you want me to put on a fake smile for you every morning, fine! I can do that! But I feel stuck in a life that I don't want."

I wanted to get away. I needed to. I felt like jumping in my car and driving until I ran out of roads. When a group of girlfriends called and invited me to attend a local punk band concert with "Captain Tractor", I jumped at the chance. It was just the thing I thought I needed.

I didn't tell Jeff where I was going.

The rocking atmosphere and deafening music brought back a kind of rebellious nostalgia. I just soaked it all up, imagining I had no obligations to anyone. I was back in college, having a reckless, rowdy party.

The place was packed and hot. I was there to have fun. Just as I was scanning the crowd, I saw *him*. He was walking straight for me. I dropped my jaw, and I'm sure I even drooled a bit. He looked so good! In fact I couldn't picture him as an adolescent anymore, and all of my memories of him were suddenly transformed into us as adults. They took on an entirely new meaning. He still had his long hair and his beautiful brown eyes, but something was definitely different. He had sex appeal! He was ripped! He had perfect teeth and a smile that spoke his intentions quite clearly. Chris. Christopher Lamage. He was here to save me.

"Phyllis!" he had the deep voice of an angel. He hadn't forgotten me. Then he hugged me. The boundary was broken. After twenty years, this moment finally replaced that stagnant meeting at the park. My imagination started churning like a swirling vortex.

"Are you here with anyone?" was his first question. I knew what he meant. It was written all over his face. He meant, "Are you attached to anyone?" He needed to know that right away. If my jaw could have dropped any further, it would have fallen on the floor. I was not that geeky eleven year-old girl to him anymore. Maybe I never had been.

"I'm just here with some girlfriends." I avoided his connotation by answering him literally. Instead, of seeming evasive, my response made him more interested.

I changed the subject to protect my vulnerability. "What have you been up to?"

He could have talked all night. I was just reveling in the moment because I knew it would be short-lived. We talked about what the band was playing. He told me about the new restaurant he had opened. It was the perfect social environment for him. He invited me to stop by sometime. I told him I definitely would. He was standing so close…

Then the time came when I had to wake up to reality. "What are you doing now?" he asked, eager for one particular answer that I couldn't give him. I pulled against the strings of integrity that held me down. Why did I have to run into him now when it was too late? If I had still been in college, I would have easily given in to my desires. I was wishing I had the cunning to lie and my evening would have been made. I was wishing I could have been the girl that he wanted me to be: the impulsive, rebellious, available girl.

Sighing, I broke the spell. I told him about my family. I showed him a picture in my wallet. His smile didn't disappear, but it became fake. He was happy for me, but disappointed at the same time. He couldn't say it, but I knew; he didn't want to "just be friends". He wanted to take me home...or maybe I just wished that he wanted to. Now, I was the untouchable one.

"That's great Phyllis." His smile was almost brotherly by now, "It was good to run into you."

"You too." I lied.

"See ya." And he was gone. He turned his back to me and disappeared in the crowd. What a beautiful back it was.

I stood there in the noise and heat feeling utterly alone. This whole night was supposed to be a return to the glory days, a chance to party without remorse, to feel young and carefree. It had backfired on me and revealed my true identity. I hated my responsibilities and my guilty conscience. I hated my husband for getting in the way. I hated him for not being Chris. I hated myself for missing the opportunity. Again.

I started hyperventilating and had to hold my hand over my mouth. I felt exhausted and trapped. Worst of all, I felt like never going back home. The churning vortex was slowly sucking me in, flashing options in front of my eyes. Like a giant magnet, I was being pulled to my car, commanded by my fierce anger to drive far away and never come back.

Then some reality kicked in. It was a mockery and a shame to have a wife and mother dancing in a bar trying to get picked up like an old cougar. I didn't belong here. I didn't belong with Chris. I couldn't explain this to the girls; they were right in front of the speakers, blinded with energy. I signalled that I was leaving and they waved, oblivious to the shame they also should feel.

As soon as I left the building, the icy night air wrapped around me and squeezed. It was so cold that I felt my lip gloss (unfortunately completely still intact) beginning to freeze. If I wasn't going back inside, where was I going? I had to assume the worst of Chris. I had to think I would have been just another fling among many. There must be some jerk of a reason why he hadn't settled down yet.

I paused. I was not going to be that jerk. It would ruin my life if I went with Chris. I would ruin my family's lives. I wanted Chris out of my brain. Out! Out! Out! I would never go to his restaurant. I would never look him up. I would never enter another den of match-making iniquity. My life at that moment changed forever.

Everyone was asleep when I snuck back in the house. The next morning I faked that I was sick and stayed in bed.

There was a soft knock on the door. Jeff came and sat on the edge of the bed.

"I'm sorry," he said, reaching to touch me, but stopped.

"What for?"

"For not being your knight in shining armour anymore. Prolonged exposure has exposed all of my hidden faults. I'm not some dreamy hunk who's never done anything wrong. I've hurt you."

His faults didn't look that bad anymore. That was the difference; I knew Jeff, and I knew I could accept him that way. I didn't know Chris at all. I hadn't known how to deal with him when we were kids and I didn't know how to deal with him now. If I could turn down a night with Chris then I could turn down a night with anyone.

Jeff was the conscious choice I had made. Even if it was reluctant loyalty, it was loyalty all the same. I had to buck up and make this marriage work. This was my moment of maturity.

"I'm the one who is hurting you. I'm sorry," I said.

My temperament seemed a permanent fixture even if my perception had changed. I still believed that Chris was the one who had got away, and I will flatter myself into thinking that he believed the same about me.

*Author's Note: Names have been changed for the hardcore protection of the innocent.

BATTLE.NET
THE PRECURSOR TO MY "IRL" DATING LIFE.
BY: HEATHER HARDIE

## The Internet and I are like old friends from middle school.

We discovered each other during our respective entries into teenage-hood; awkwardly yet eagerly exploring the uncharted territories of Napster, Yahoo! mail, Geocities "homepages" and early chat rooms.

Meet the Internet circa 1996: a naive, blossoming interweb of rudimentary html, dancing baby animations, dial-up connections and **Comic Sans**. A network still commonly referred to as the World Wide Web; not yet infiltrated with popups, advertising, social networking sites or wikis.

A world so new that issues of identity and security were hardly considered; a brutal truth attributing directly to my unbridled fixation with talking to strangers online. Unbeknownst to my parents, I was knee-deep in sketchy internet relationships, imaginary dating scenarios and cyber sex, all by the tender age of 12.

Before the chatting phenomena that were mIRC and ICQ, (which, for those of you who are *really* young, preceded MSN Messenger and Skype and whatever other newfangled chatting programs you kids use these days) I discovered an online community called

# BATTLE.NET

Battle.net was the online interface that connected users of *Diablo,* which is a role playing game (*RPG*) set in dark, dungeon-y, dragon-y fantasy worlds. Now let's be clear: I am, and never was invested in *gaming* to the extent that I would refer to myself as a *gamer.*

This is not some cheap attempt at saving face, because believe me, I consider myself a geek in other ways (knitting circle, anyone?). To me, Battle.net was an accessible social tool allowing me to freely "meet" people and explore what it meant to be in a "relationship".

The setup at Battle.net was, from what I remember, a main page of common chat rooms where users would meet and discuss things like how to defeat the boss dragon at the end of level 13 or the cheat for unlimited potions, magical swords and what-have-you. One could also create a private, password-protected chat room for more "intimate" conversations. They were also used for guild meetings and other game-related strategies, I guess.

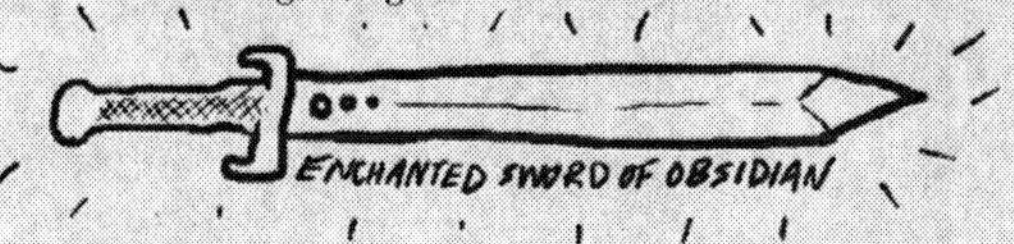

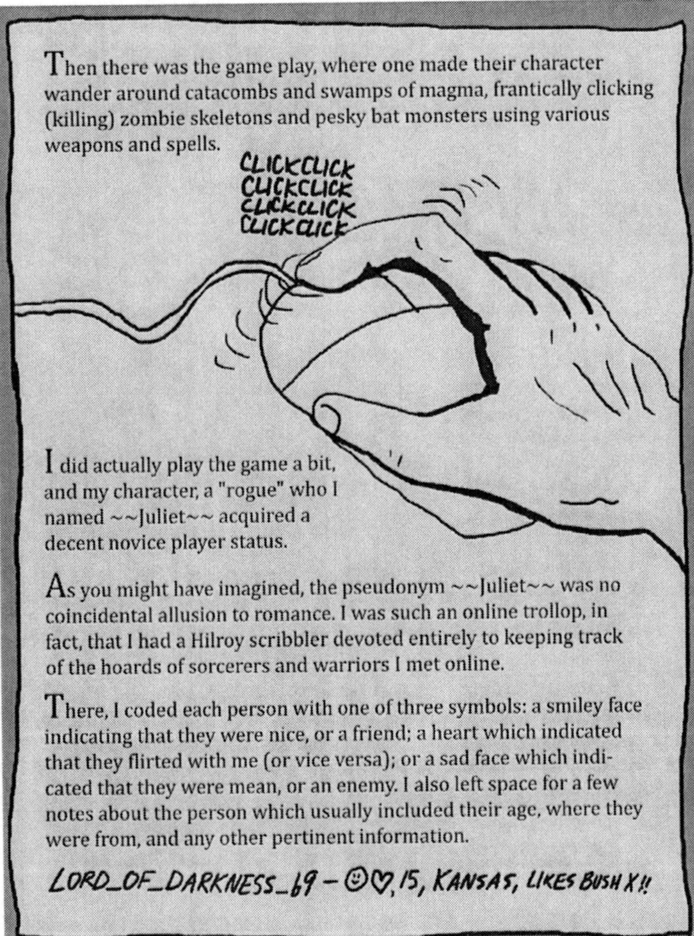
Then there was the game play, where one made their character wander around catacombs and swamps of magma, frantically clicking (killing) zombie skeletons and pesky bat monsters using various weapons and spells.
CLICKCLICK
CLICKCLICK
CLICKCLICK
CLICKCLICK
I did actually play the game a bit, and my character, a "rogue" who I named ~~Juliet~~ acquired a decent novice player status.
As you might have imagined, the pseudonym ~~Juliet~~ was no coincidental allusion to romance. I was such an online trollop, in fact, that I had a Hilroy scribbler devoted entirely to keeping track of the hoards of sorcerers and warriors I met online.
There, I coded each person with one of three symbols: a smiley face indicating that they were nice, or a friend; a heart which indicated that they flirted with me (or vice versa); or a sad face which indicated that they were mean, or an enemy. I also left space for a few notes about the person which usually included their age, where they were from, and any other pertinent information.
LORD_OF_DARKNESS_69 – ☺♡, 15, KANSAS, LIKES BUSH X!!

On that note, personal information was, even then, taken with a grain of salt. However, I prided myself on being honest about "everything except my age and my bra size", which I told people were "16 and 34C".

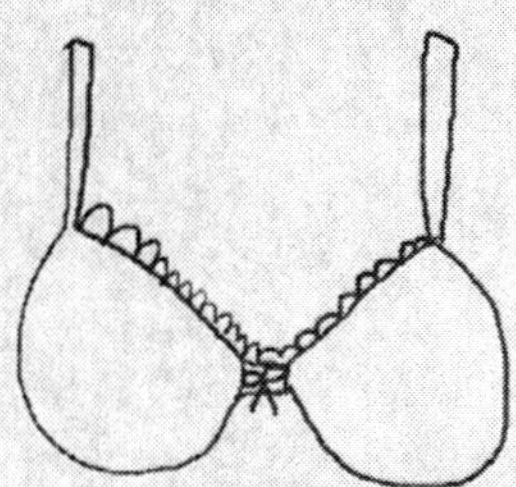

Disclosing real information like one's name was almost unnecessary - people were actually content to accept that Battle.net was a life outside of real life. Even emails and photos weren't exchanged, at least not often, and so we operated solely with our vivid imaginations and early manifestations of emoticons and chat lingo.

## @>--}---- This was a popular pick-up tactic. The rose.

Anyway, without going into graphic detail, these online relationships would begin and end almost like real ones: awkward first dates, first kisses, weddings, the works. I kid you not, I have attended several Battle.net weddings. Divorces happened too. There were hot tub parties, dinner parties, you name it.

I vividly remember a romantic date where my boyfriend, Rave1 and I got ice cream together, walked in the rain and shared a sweet, ice cream kiss under a gazebo. I think there might have been a rainbow, too. It was easy to get sucked into this artificial world, not unlike World of Warcraft addicts today.

Just once, I was convinced to talk on the phone with one of my more serious Battle.net boyfriends. His real name was Pete and he spoke in a stereotypically nasal, geek voice. That experience slightly shattered the romantic, frosted window that obscured my perceptions of the strangers I chatted with online.

I knew full well that people lied about who they were, but I could tell which ones were, like me, fudging the facts by a few notches, and which ones were *really* lying. For example, in an intimate moment, when someone says, "I want to rip open your blouse and expose your full bosoms", you can sort of tell it's not a 14 year old from New Jersey you're talking to.

That being said, I didn't bother getting hung up on real life truths, because they had nothing to do with life on Battle.net. I was pretty sure that Rave1 was not actually who he said he was, but we still had amazing eight hour conversations and terribly cute, imaginary dating scenarios. It was like *actually being with someone*; we would talk, and act out how it would be if we were actually together. For example:

**Enter chat room RaveOn.** (That was our private room that I cleverly made up.)

**Rave1 says:** Jules, I missed you! How was your day? *takes you into my arms and hugs tightly*

**~~Juliet~~ says:** I missed you too! It was ok, but I'm so tired and glad to be here with you. *looks up and kisses you lightly on the cheek*

**Rave1 says:** You look so beautiful. Are you hungry? I made dinner. *leads you to the table and kisses your neck as you sit down*

**~~Juliet~~ says:** Starving! Oh it smells delicious! I love spaghetti. *starts eating*

**Rave1 says:** *watches fondly while you eat*

You see, it wasn't always nasty, 40-something year olds pretending to be 16, typing horrific, porn-y things at me all the time. It was mundane yet heartfelt crap, most of which actually does happen in real life relationships.

So when I say that Battle.net was a precursor to my *real* dating life, it absolutely was. I learned about flirting there (and I *still* find flirting online much easier than in person), and most importantly, about communication.

Besides online boyfriends I had a lot of online friends, and we talked about music, hobbies, school, and personal things like depression and family problems.

The delay between reading what someone said and typing out a response allowed for more thoughtful, deliberate conversation. The absence of real life insecurities made for honest, open expression.

I feel that because of these early online relationships I now have a knack for deciding if someone is a good match for me based on our conversations. I place importance on the use of language, and I tend to ignore outwardly projected characteristics like physical appearance and clothing until I get a feel for how we communicate, and if we actually "click" that way.

This is not to say that I don't notice attractive people, or will date an ugly person just because we can carry out a nice conversation, (because I've tried that and it *does not work.)*

**On Battle.net, a person's actual appearance was irrelevant because we just lied about that stuff anyway.**

In real life (IRL) one can lie *to an extent* by acting and dressing a certain way, but, as with creepy people online, most people can see through that facade, if not right away then hopefully *before* meeting innocently at the local library and winding up eating spiders in a **real life dungeon** in some lonely sociopath's basement.

I'm glad I honed my creep-detecting skills early on in life, and engaged in safe, trial-runs of dating before going out into the real world.

**Thanks Battle.net!**

# A Reading Group Guide

## Questions and topics for discussion

---

1. All the stories in *Living Apart Together: A New Possibility for Loving Couples* describe real life scenarios. Do you know anyone who lives in a LAT relationship? Has reading the accounts in this anthology changed the way you think about this lifestyle? Is a LAT relationship one that you might have chosen at an earlier time in your life? Is it an option you would consider now? What factors are most important for deciding whether it is a reasonable choice for a couple?

2. The couples in *Living Apart Together: A New Possibility for Loving Couples* are financially able to manage two households. British actress Helena Bonham Carter and director Tim Burton live in adjoining townhouses in London. Each place is decorated to suit the respec-

tive personality and there is a room between the two. "To me, it makes complete sense," Bonham Carter says. "If you've got some money, and you can afford it, why not have your own space?" Is this lifestye just another option available only for the well-off?

3. Studies show that seniors sixty and older (baby boomers) are much more likely than previous cohorts to be part of a LAT couple. Sociologists think that LAT arrangements play a profound role in the well-being of seniors. Why do you think this age group might not want the constraints of a shared address?

4. *In Love in the Time of Swine Flu,* Ann Rourke describes reconnecting with an old high school sweetheart. Initially they are caught up in the excitement of being in love. Neither seems to recognize how they have grown and changed. Have you ever reconnected with a former lover? In what way did you acknowledge the way each of you has changed? Do you think Ann and Ted could have worked out a way to be together but apart? If so, how? If not, why? Does it seem that more women than men are interested in living in a LAT?

5. Jody Jeannine's "An International Love Story," describes a LAT marriage that bridges two countries on different sides of the world and in which school aged children are being raised. What are the many benefits described by the writer for the parent-child and spousal relationship to their arrangement? How feasible do you think a LAT is for a young couple raising children?

6. In *Love with Antonio* the writer describes a thirty-three year relationship. In her account of the first

two decades of their LAT, she writes of the pressure from friends to live together and about suggestions that she is being used by a man. How does one counteract the social pressures that urge women to accept traditional living arrangements?

7. Proponents of LAT marriages suggest that living apart without the trials and intimacies of cohabitation keeps romance alive. They observe contemporary relationships where partners are semi-happy without romance. Do you think a LAT arrangement makes for a more alive and richer relationship?

8. Critics of LATs cite disadvantages to living apart: Sex and companionship are less readily available, and such couples miss the shared creativity that comes with making a home. Moreover, they will have less of an opportunity to create or try to replicate their original family closeness. Living together forces partners to navigate the ups and downs of everyday issues. Living apart could mean the partners are afraid of being truly intimate. What do you think of these criticisms?

# About the Editors

British Columbia-raised Linda Breault holds degrees from the University of British Columbia, University of Victoria and Simon Fraser University. Her careers in Canada span a lifetime of work with young people and women, but her joy is in international work supporting marginalized people in self-development and self-reliance. Her work has taken her to Africa, Latin America, New Zealand, Central Asia and China. A single parent, she raised two children and is the proud grandmother of four.

Dianne Gillespie grew up in Ontario and the prairies. She earned her degrees at York University and the University of Victoria. She has been a secondary English teacher in British Columbia for over thirty years. With a love of travel, she worked at an international school in China, where she met Linda. She is passionate about promoting literacy. Happily partnered, she is the mother of two grown daughters.

Linda and Dianne can be reached through breault.gillespietba@gmail.com and at http://www.livingapart-togetherlat.com/

*Linda Breault*

*Dianne Gillespie*

CPSIA information can be obtained at www.ICGtesting.com
Printed in the USA
LVOW11s0927281115

464483LV00001B/50/P